It's another Quality Book from CGP

This book is for anyone doing Edexcel Modular GCSE Maths
at Higher Level.

It contains lots of tricky questions designed
to make you sweat — because that's the only
way you'll get any better.

It's also got some daft bits in to try and make
the whole experience at least vaguely
entertaining for you.

What CGP is all about

Our sole aim here at CGP is to produce the highest quality
books — carefully written, immaculately presented and
dangerously close to being funny.

Then we work our socks off to get them out to you
— at the cheapest possible prices.

Contents

Stage One

Stage Two

Stage Three

Published by Coordination Group Publications Ltd.
Illustrated by Ruso Bradley, Lex Ward and Ashley Tyson

Coordinated by June Hall and Mark Haslam

Contributors:
Philip Wood
Margaret Carr
Barbara Coleman
John Lyons
Gordon Rutter
Claire Thompson

Updated by:
Peter Caunter
Alison Chisholm
Philippa Falshaw
Sharon Keeley
Tim Major
Sam Norman
Glenn Rogers
Julie Wakeling
Sharon Watson

ISBN 1 84146 091 5

Groovy website: www.cgpbooks.co.uk

Printed by Elanders Hindson, Newcastle upon Tyne.
Clipart sources: CorelDRAW and VECTOR.

Numbers

Q1 Sarah thinks of a number. She calculates that the square of the number is 256. What is the square root of the number Sarah thought of originally?

Q2 On a certain day the temperature at midday was 14 °C. By midnight the temperature had fallen by 17 °C. What was the temperature at midnight?

Q3 A school ran three evening classes: <u>judo</u>, <u>karate</u> and <u>kendo</u>. The judo class had 29 pupils, the karate class had 27 and the kendo class 23.
For which classes did the teacher have difficulty dividing the pupils into equal groups?

Q4 The number one is the first odd number. It is also the first square number, the first cube number and the first triangle number.
a) Which is greater: the third odd number, the third square number or the third cube number?
b) Write down the prime factors of the third triangle number.

There are five special number sequences that you really need to know:
EVEN, ODD, SQUARE, CUBE and TRIANGLE NUMBERS.

Q5 The following sequences are described in words. Write down their first four terms.
a) The prime numbers starting from 17.
b) The squares of odd numbers starting from $9^2 = 81$.
c) The triangular numbers starting from 15.

Remember — 1 is not a prime. Look, it just isn't, OK.

Q6 Using any or all of the figures **1, 2, 5, 9** write down:
a) the smallest prime number
b) a prime number greater than 20
c) a prime number between 10 and 20
d) two prime numbers whose sum is 21
e) a number that is not prime.

Q7 **a)** In the ten by ten square opposite, ring all the <u>prime numbers</u>.
(The first three have been done for you.)
b) Among the prime numbers between 10 and 100, find three which are still prime when their digits are reversed.
c) Give a reason for 27 not being a prime number.

1	②	③	4	⑤	6	7	8	9	10
11	12	13	14	15	16	17	18	19	20
21	22	23	24	25	26	27	28	29	30
31	32	33	34	35	36	37	38	39	40
41	42	43	44	45	46	47	48	49	50
51	52	53	54	55	56	57	58	59	60
61	62	63	64	65	66	67	68	69	70
71	72	73	74	75	76	77	78	79	80
81	82	83	84	85	86	87	88	89	90
91	92	93	94	95	96	97	98	99	100

Q8 What is the largest prime less than 300?

Q9 How many prime numbers are even?

This stuff <u>keeps coming up</u> in the Exam — so make sure you can check if a number's prime or not. It's actually dead easy — check out the method in the Revision Guide.

Factors and Primes

Q1   1   3   6   9   12

From the numbers above, write down:

a) a multiple of 4

b) the prime number

c) two square numbers

d) three factors of 27

e) two numbers P and Q that satisfy both $P = 2Q$ and $P = \sqrt{144}$

Q2   Find the lowest common multiple of: **a)** 5 and 9   **b)** 4 and 6   **c)** 4, 6 and 8

Find the highest common factor of: **d)** 26 and 52   **e)** 26, 39 and 52

Q3 **a)** Write down the first ten triangle numbers.

b) From your list pick out all the multiples of 2.

c) From your list pick out all the multiples of 3.

d) From your list pick out any prime numbers.

e) Add the numbers in your list together and write down the prime factorisation of the total.

The clue's in the question...

Q4 **a)** Write down the first five cube numbers.

b) Which of the numbers given in part **a)** are multiples of 2?

c) Which of the numbers given in part **a)** are multiples of 3?

d) Which of the numbers given in part **a)** are multiples of 4?

e) Which of the numbers given in part **a)** are multiples of 5?

Q5 **a)** List the first five odd numbers.

b) If added together, what is their total?

c) Write down the prime factorisation of the answer to part **b)**.

Q6 **a)** List the first five prime numbers.

b) If added together, what is their total?

c) Write down the prime factorisation of the answer to part **b)**.

Q7   Bryan and Sue were playing a guessing game. Sue thought of a number between 1 and 100 which Bryan had to guess. Bryan was allowed to ask five questions, which are listed with Sue's responses in the table below.

Bryan's Questions	Sue's Responses
Is it prime?	No
Is it odd?	No
Is it less than 50?	Yes
Is it a multiple of 3?	Yes
Is it a multiple of 7?	Yes

Start by writing down a number table up to 100. Look at each response in turn and cross off numbers 'till you've only got one left.

What is the number that Sue thought of?

Rounding Off & Estimating

Rounding a number off to a certain number of decimal places or significant figures is really quite easy — the tricky bit's when they ask for minimum and maximum values...

Q1 *K* = 456.9873

Write *K* correct to:

a) one decimal place
b) two decimal places
c) three decimal places

d) three significant figures
e) two significant figures
f) one significant figure.

Q2 Without using your calculator find approximate answers to the following:

a) 6560 × 1.97
b) 8091 × 1.456
c) 38.45 × 1.4237 × 5.0002
d) 45.34 ÷ 9.345
e) 34504 ÷ 7133
f) $\dfrac{55.33 \times 19.345}{9.23}$

g) 7139 × 2.13
h) 98 × 2.54 × 2.033
i) 21 × 21 × 21
j) 8143 ÷ 81
k) 62000 ÷ 950
l) π ÷ 3

Q3 Estimate the area under the graph.

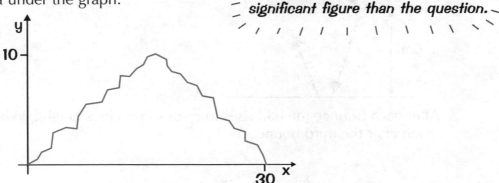

Always give your answer to one less significant figure than the question.

Q4 A supermarket chain sold 14 634 tins of beans during a four-week period.
a) If the supermarkets were open every day of the week, how many days did it take to sell the 14 634 tins of beans?
b) What was the average number of tins of beans sold each day?
c) Show your working for a rough estimate to **b)** to check that your answer is of the right order of magnitude.

"of the right order of magnitude" is just a posh way of saying "the right size", by the way.

Q5 π is the number of times that the diameter of a circle divides into the circumference. Many values have been used as estimates — here are a few examples:

$$3, \quad \frac{22}{7}, \quad \sqrt{10}, \quad \frac{255}{81}, \quad 3\frac{17}{120}.$$

a) Use your calculator to give each estimate correct to 7 decimal places.
b) Which is the most accurate estimate for π?

Fractions

Q1 Evaluate the following, giving your answer as a fraction in its lowest terms:

a) $\dfrac{1}{2}+\dfrac{1}{4}$

e) $6\times\dfrac{2}{3}$

i) $3+\dfrac{8}{5}$

b) $\dfrac{2}{3}-\dfrac{1}{4}$

f) $\dfrac{4}{5}\div\dfrac{2}{3}$

j) $\dfrac{2}{3}\left(\dfrac{3}{4}+\dfrac{4}{5}\right)$

c) $\dfrac{1}{5}+\dfrac{2}{3}-\dfrac{2}{5}$

g) $\dfrac{5}{12}\times\dfrac{3}{2}$

k) $\left(\dfrac{1}{7}+\dfrac{3}{14}\right)\times\left(3-\dfrac{1}{5}\right)$

d) $5-\dfrac{1}{4}$

h) $\dfrac{5}{6}-\dfrac{7}{8}$

l) $\left(\dfrac{3}{4}-\dfrac{1}{5}\right)\div\left(\dfrac{7}{8}+\dfrac{1}{16}\right)$

Q2 Dwight scored 50 goals last season. 30 of these were scored at his home ground.
a) Write down the fraction (in its lowest terms) of goals scored at his home ground.
b) Calculate the fraction of goals scored away from home.

Q3 A ball is dropped from a height of 6 m.

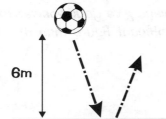

6m

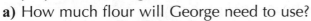

After each bounce the ball rises to $\dfrac{2}{3}$ of its previous height. What height will it reach after the third bounce?

Q4 George wants to make a cake. The recipe requires 150 g each of flour, sugar and butter, and 3 eggs. George only has 2 eggs so he decides to make a smaller cake with the same proportions of ingredients.

a) How much flour will George need to use?
b) If each egg weighs 25 g, how much will the cake weigh before it goes in the oven?
c) What fraction of the uncooked weight is flour?
d) If the cake loses one seventh of its weight during baking (due to moisture loss) what will it weigh after baking?

Q5 The population of Australia is 18 million, of which 3.5 million people live in Sydney and 1 million people live in Perth.
a) What fraction of the population live in Perth?
b) What fraction of the population live in Perth or Sydney?

Decimals

Q1   Write the following fractions as decimals:

a) $\dfrac{3}{10}$ b) $\dfrac{37}{100}$ c) $\dfrac{2}{5}$ d) $\dfrac{3}{8}$

e) $\dfrac{14}{8}$ f) $\dfrac{8}{64}$ g) $\dfrac{24}{40}$ h) $\dfrac{4}{80}$

Q2   Write the following decimals as fractions in their lowest form:

a) 0.6   b) 0.75   c) 0.95   d) 0.128

e) $0.\dot{3}$ f) $0.\dot{6}$ g) $0.\dot{1}$ h) $0.1\dot{6}$

Q3   Fill in the gaps in the following conversion table :

Fraction	Decimal
½	0.5
⅕	
	0.125
	1.6
⁴⁄16	
⁷⁄2	
	0.x
ˣ⁄100	
³⁄20	
	0.45

   Decimals are just another way of writing fractions —
so it's easy to convert between the two...

Q4   Write the following recurring decimals as fractions in their lowest form:

a) 0.666...   b) 0.444...   c) 0.888...   d) 0.808080...

e) 0.121212...   f) 0.545545545...   g) 0.753753753...   h) 0.156156156...

Q5   Write the following fractions as recurring decimals:

a) $\dfrac{5}{6}$ b) $\dfrac{7}{9}$ c) $\dfrac{7}{11}$ d) $\dfrac{47}{99}$

e) $\dfrac{10}{11}$ f) $\dfrac{29}{33}$ g) $\dfrac{478}{999}$ h) $\dfrac{5891}{9999}$

Calculator Buttons

Q1 Using the x^2 button on your calculator, work out:

a) 1^2 **d)** 16^2 **g)** $(-5)^2$

b) 2^2 **e)** $(-1)^2$ **h)** 1000^2

c) 11^2 **f)** 30^2 **i)** 0^2

(For parts **e)** and **g)** use your $+/-$ button too)

Q2 Using the $\sqrt{}$ button on your calculator, work out:

a) $\sqrt{16}$ **d)** $\sqrt{0}$ **g)** $\sqrt{3}$

b) $\sqrt{36}$ **e)** $\sqrt{3600}$ **h)** $\sqrt{7}$

c) $\sqrt{289}$ **f)** $\sqrt{400}$ **i)** $\sqrt{30}$

Q3 Use the $\sqrt[3]{}$ button on your calculator to work out:

a) $\sqrt[3]{1}$ **e)** $\sqrt[3]{27}$

b) $\sqrt[3]{0}$ **f)** $\sqrt[3]{-27}$

c) $\sqrt[3]{343}$ **g)** $\sqrt[3]{-64}$

d) $\sqrt[3]{1000}$ **h)** $\sqrt[3]{-5}$

Yeah, OK, we all know how to do sums on a calculator — but it can do so much more... check out the groovy powers button and the funky brackets buttons, not to mention the slinky $1/x$ button...

Q4 By calculating the bottom line first (the denominator) and then using your calculator's memory buttons (Min or STO and MR or RCL), work out:

a) $\dfrac{21}{2+\sin 30°}$ **c)** $\dfrac{15}{\cos 30°+22}$ **e)** $\dfrac{12}{12+\tan 60°}$

b) $\dfrac{\tan 15°}{12+12^2}$ **d)** $\dfrac{18}{3+\sqrt[3]{12}}$ **f)** $\dfrac{18}{11+\tan 77°}$

Q5 Using $[(---$ and $---)]$, calculate:

Here comes BODMAS...

a) $\dfrac{(14+18)}{(2\times 8)}$ **c)** $\dfrac{(9+(4\div 2))}{(11\times 3)}$ **e)** $\dfrac{12}{(8+9)(13-11)}$

b) $\dfrac{8}{(1\times 4)(8-6)}$ **d)** $\dfrac{14(4\times 8)}{(6+9)}$ **f)** $\dfrac{7(5+4)}{12(9\times 8)}$

Q6 Using the x^y button, find:

a) 2^0 **d)** π^2 **g)** $(\cos 30°)^5$

b) 4^{10} **e)** e^3 **h)** 4.29^7

c) 2^{20} **f)** 3^{10} **i)** $(\sin 45°)^4$

Conversion Factors and Metric & Imperial Units

You've got to know all the metric and imperial conversion factors — there's no way out of it, you'll just have to sit down and learn them, sorry and all that...

Q1   Express the given quantity in the unit(s) in brackets:

a) 2 m [cm]	**g)** 87 in [ft and in]	**m)** 6 ft [in]	**s)** 8 cm 6 mm [mm]
b) 3.3 cm [mm]	**h)** 43 oz [lb and oz]	**n)** 5 lb [oz]	**t)** 3 ft 6 in [in]
c) 4 kg [g]	**i)** 650 m [km]	**o)** 301 ft [yd and ft]	**u)** 4 lb 7 oz [oz]
d) 600 g [kg]	**j)** 9 kg [g]	**p)** 6 m [mm]	**v)** 550 kg [t]
e) 4 ft [in]	**k)** 7 g [kg]	**q)** 2 t [kg]	**w)** 3 m 54 cm [cm]
f) 36 in [ft]	**l)** 950 g [kg]	**r)** 3000 g [kg]	**x)** 0.7 cm [mm]

Q2   Deborah weighs 9 stone 4 pounds.
There are 14 pounds in a stone and 1 kilogram is equal to 0.157 stone.
Change Deborah's weight into kilograms.

Q3   A horse's drinking trough holds 14 gallons of water.
Approximately how many litres is this?

Q4   Convert 147 g into ounces.

Q5   Barbara cycled 51 km in one day while Barry cycled 30 miles. Who cycled further?

Q6   A pile of bricks weighs 7 metric tonnes. Approximately how many imperial tons is this?

Q7   A seamstress needs to cut an 11 inch strip of finest Chinese silk.
a) Approximately how many cm is this?
b) Approximately how many mm is this?

Q8   At the gym Arnold can lift a barbell weighing 60 kg.
a) Approximately how many lbs is this?
b) How many ounces is this?
Sylvester can lift a barbell weighing 0.059 tonnes.
c) Who can lift the most?

Q9   A recipe for The World's Wobbliest Jelly requires 5 lb of sugar. How many 1 kg bags of sugar does Dick need to buy so that he can make a jelly?

Q10   Neil is going to buy some fabric for a new pair of trousers that he is going to make. A local shop prices the fabric that he would like at £9.84 per square yard. A fabric superstore prices the same fabric at £10.80 per square metre. According to price, where should Neil buy his fabric? (Use the conversion factor 91 cm = 1 yard.)

Q11   The priceless Greek statue in my garden is 21 feet tall.

a) How many inches is this?
b) How many yards is this?
c) How many metres is this?
d) How many cm is this?
e) How many mm is this?
f) How many km is this?

Conversion Factors and Metric & Imperial Units

Q12 Convert the following into hours and minutes:

    a) 3.25 hours   **b)** 0.4 hours   **c)** 7.3 hours   **d)** 1.2 hours.

Q13 The Bon Voyage Holiday Company are offering an exchange rate of 1.48 euros for £1 sterling. They are also offering 11.03 Danish kroner for £1 sterling and 2.45 Australian dollars for £1 sterling. Calculate, to the nearest penny, the sterling equivalent of:

    a) 220 euros   **g)** 899 Danish kroner

    b) 686 Danish kroner   **h)** 20 euros

    c) 1664 Australian dollars   **i)** 668 Australian dollars

    d) 148 euros   **j)** 3389 Danish kroner

    e) 15 Danish kroner   **k)** 1000 Australian dollars

    f) 1950 Australian dollars   **l)** 1 euro

Q14

> **1 pint = 0.568 litres**
> **£1 = \$1.42**

Which is better value, 2 pints of beer for \$5.76 or 1 litre of beer for £3.92?

Q15 The scale on a map is 1:10 000.
How big are the following in real life:

    a) a distance of 2 cm on the map

    b) a distance of 20 cm on the map

    c) a distance of 70 cm on the map

    d) an area of 2 cm^2 on the map?

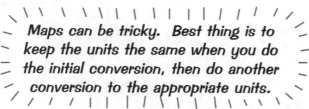

Maps can be tricky. Best thing is to keep the units the same when you do the initial conversion, then do another conversion to the appropriate units.

Q16 Another map has a scale of 1:3000.
What size on this map are the following:

    a) a distance of 5 km in real life

    b) a distance of 1 km in real life

    c) an area of 100 m^2 in real life

    d) an area of 50 m^2 in real life?

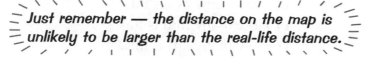

Just remember — the distance on the map is unlikely to be larger than the real-life distance.

Ratios

I don't want to spoil the surprise, but you're going to need your calculator for this bit — get your finger on that fraction button...

RATIOS are like FRACTIONS which are like DECIMALS

We can treat the RATIO 3:4 like the FRACTION $\frac{3}{4}$, which is 0.75 as a DECIMAL.

Watch out though — this <u>isn't</u> $\frac{3}{4}$ of the <u>total</u>:

If there are girls and boys in the ratio 3:4, it means there's $\frac{3}{4}$ as many girls as boys.

So if there's 8 boys, there's $\frac{3}{4} \times 8 = 6$ girls.

Q1 Write these ratios in their simplest forms:
- **a)** 6:8
- **b)** 5:20
- **c)** 1.5:3
- **d)** 2¼: 4
- **e)** 2 weeks: 4 days
- **f)** £1.26:14p

Q2 A rectangle has sides in the ratio 1:2. Calculate the length of the longer side if the shorter side is:
- **a)** 3 cm
- **b)** 5.5 cm
- **c)** 15.2 m

Calculate the length of the shorter side if the longer side is:
- **d)** 3 cm
- **e)** 5.5 cm
- **f)** 15.2 m

Q3 Divide the following amounts in the ratios given:
- **a)** £20 in the ratio 2:3
- **b)** 150 m in the ratio 8:7
- **c)** 500 g in the ratio 1:2:2
- **d)** 8 hrs in the ratio 1:2:3

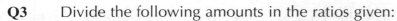

For questions like this — you add up the ratio numbers to find the total number of parts and <u>divide</u> by this. Then <u>multiply</u> by each number in the ratio separately to find the different amounts.

Q4
- **a)** <u>Increase</u> £3.20 in the ratio 2:3.
- **b)** <u>Decrease</u> 120 cm in the ratio 3:2.

Q5 John and Peter share a bar of chocolate marked into 16 squares. They share it in the ratio 1:3. How many squares does each boy get?

Q6

A 2 litre bottle of cola is to be shared between three girls in the ratio 2:3:5. How many <u>millilitres</u> will each girl get?

<u>Watch out for your units</u> — you'll have to change them over for this one — and your answer should be in <u>millilitres</u>.

Q7 Oak and ash saplings are planted along a roadside in the ratio 2:3 respectively. If there are 20 oak saplings, how many ash saplings are there?

Q8 Tony gives £100 to be shared by Jane, Paul and Rosemary in ratio according to their <u>age</u>. Jane is 10, Paul is 12 and Rosemary 3 years old. How much will each child get?

Percentages

Make sure you can switch from fractions to decimals to percentages before you start.

Q1 Express each percentage as a decimal:

a) 50%   **b)** 12%   **c)** 40%   **d)** 34%

Q2 Express each percentage as a fraction in its lowest terms:

a) 25%   **b)** 60%   **c)** 45%   **d)** 30%

Q3 Express each of the following as a percentage:

a) $\dfrac{1}{8}$ **b)** 0.23   **c)** $\dfrac{12}{40}$ **d)** 0.34

Q4 In a French test, Lauren scored 17/20. What percentage is this?

Q5 87 out of 120 pupils at Backwater School have access to a computer. What percentage is this?

There are three types of percentage question. The first one is working out "something % of something else" — it's dead easy. Just remember to add it back on to the original amount if you've got a VAT question.

Q6

Four friends stay at the Pickled Parrot Hotel for a night and each take an evening meal. Bed and Breakfast costs £37 per person and the evening meal costs £15 per person. How much is the total cost, if VAT is added at 17½%?

Q7 John bought a new video recorder. The tag in the shop said it cost £299 + VAT. If VAT is charged at 17½%, how much did he pay (to the nearest penny)?

Q8 Donald earns an annual wage of £23 500. He doesn't pay tax on the first £3400 that he earns. How much income tax does he pay a year if the rate of tax is:

a) 25%

b) 40%?

Q9 Tanya paid £6500 for her new car. Each year its value decreased by 8%.
a) How much was it worth when it was one year old?
b) How much was it worth when it was two years old?

Q10 Jeremy wanted a new sofa for his lounge. A local furniture shop had just what he was looking for — and for only £130.00 + VAT. Jeremy had £150 pounds in his bank account. If VAT was charged at 17½%, could Jeremy afford the sofa?

Here's the 2ⁿᵈ type — finding "something as a percentage of something else" — in this case you're looking at percentage change, so don't forget to work that out first.

Q11 During a rainstorm, a water butt increased in weight from 10.4 kg to 13.6 kg. What was the percentage increase (to the nearest per cent)?

Percentages

Q12 There are approximately 6000 fish and chip shops in the UK. On average, a fish and chip shop gets about 160 visitors each day. Given that the population of the UK is roughly 60 million, approximately what percentage of the population visit a fish and chip shop each day?

Q13 An electrical store reduces the price of a particular camera from £90.00 to £78.30. What is the percentage reduction (to 1 d.p.)?

Q14 I wish to invest £1000 for a period of three years and have decided to place my money with the Highrise Building Society on 1 January. If I choose to use the Gold Account I will withdraw the interest at the end of each year. If I choose to use the Silver Account I will leave the interest to be added to the capital at the end of each year.

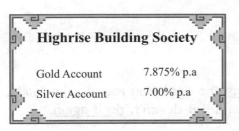

Highrise Building Society

Gold Account   7.875% p.a

Silver Account   7.00% p.a

a) Calculate the total interest I will receive if I use the Gold Account.

b) Calculate the total interest I will receive if I use the Silver Account.

After some thought I decide to use the Gold Account and leave the interest to be added to the capital at the end of each year.

c) Calculate the total interest I will now receive from the Gold Account.

Q15 At birth, Veronica was 0.3 m tall. By adulthood she had grown to 1.5 m tall. Calculate her height now as a percentage of her height at birth.

Q16 Desmond's GCSE maths exam is next week. As part of his revision he attempted 31 questions on his least favourite topic of percentages. He got 21 questions fully right on the first attempt. Two days later he tried all 31 questions again and this time got 29 correct.

a) What percentage of questions did he get correct on his first attempt?

b) What percentage of questions did he get correct on his second attempt?

c) What is the percentage improvement in Desmond's results?

Q17 If $L = MN$, what is the percentage increase in L if M increases by 15% and N increases by 20%?

Ooh... here's the 3ʳᵈ type — finding the original value. The bit most people get wrong is deciding whether the value given represents more or less than 100% of the original — so always check your answer makes sense.

Q18 In the new year sales Robin bought a tennis racket for £68.00. The original price had been reduced by 15%. What was the original price?

Q19 There are 360 people living in a certain village. The population of the village has grown by 20% over the past year.

a) How many people lived in the village one year ago?

b) If the village continues to grow at the same rate, how many whole years from today will it be before the population is more than twice its current size?

Growth and Decay

Hey look — it's another of those "there is only one formula to learn and you use it for every question" topics.

So I reckon you'd better learn **The Formula** then...

Q1 Calculate the amount in each account if:
  a) £200 is invested for 10 years at 9% compound interest per annum
  b) £500 is invested for 3 years at 7% compound interest per annum
  c) £750 is invested for 30 months at 8% compound interest per annum
  d) £1000 is invested for 15 months at 6.5% compound interest per annum.

Q2 A colony of bacteria grows at the compound rate of 12% per hour.
  Initially there are 200 bacteria.
  a) How many will there be after 3 hours?
  b) How many will there be after 1 day?
  c) After how many whole hours will there be at least 4000 bacteria? (Solve this by trial and error.)

Just make sure you get the **increase** and **decrease** the right way round... basically, just check your answer sounds like you'd expect — and if it doesn't, **do it again**.

Q3 A radioactive element was observed every day and the mass remaining was measured. Initially there was 9 kg, but this decreased at the compound rate of 3% per day. How much radioactive element will be left after:
  a) 3 days
  b) 6 days
  c) 1 week
  d) 4 weeks?
  Give your answer to no more than 3 d.p.

Q4 Money is invested on the stock market. During a recession the value of the shares fall by 2% per week.
  Find the value of the stock if:
  a) £2000 was invested for a fortnight
  b) £30,000 was invested for four weeks
  c) £500 was invested for 7 weeks
  d) £100,000 was invested for a year.

Q5 Mrs Smith decides to invest £7000 in a savings account. She has the choice of putting all her money into an account paying 5% compound interest per annum or she can put half of her investment into an instant account paying 6% compound interest per annum and the remaining half into an instant access account paying 4% per annum.
  If she left the investment alone for 3 years, which is her best option and by how much?

I'd put my money in Victorian rolling pins, myself...

Growth and Decay

Q6 The activity of a radio-isotope decreases at a compound rate of 9% every hour. If the initial activity is recorded at 1100 counts per minute, what will it be after:

a) 2 hours

b) 4 hours

c) 1 day?

d) The activity of the same radio-isotope is recorded at just 66 counts per minute. Using trial and error, estimate the length of time elapsed since the recording of 1100 counts per minute.

Q7 A car is estimated to depreciate in value by 14% each year. Find the estimated values of these used cars:

a) a Peugeot 206 which cost £8,495 six months ago

b) a BMW which cost £34,000 eighteen months ago

c) a Volvo S40 which cost £13,495 two years ago

d) a Vauxhall Vectra which cost £14,395 two years ago

e) a Ford Escort which cost £11,295 three years ago

f) a Daewoo Nexia which cost £6,795 twelve months ago.

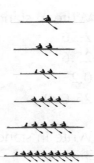

Q8 An antique vase has increased in value since its owner bought it five years ago at £220. If its value has appreciated by 16% per year, how much is it worth today?

Q9 Property prices in one area have depreciated in value by 5% per year. Calculate the expected value today of these properties:

a) a house bought for £45,000, 3 years ago

b) a bungalow bought for £58,000, 4 years ago

c) a flat bought for £52,000, six months ago

d) a factory bought for £350,000, 7 years ago.

Q10 A company owns machinery which cost £3,500 four years ago. The depreciation has been 2½% per year. What is the machinery's second-hand value today?

Q11 A culture of bacteria increases in number at a compound rate of 0.4% per hour. If initially there was a culture of 50 cells, how many cells will there be after:

a) 3 hours

b) 8 hours 30 minutes

c) 135 mins

d) 2 days?

Q12 The population of a country is 16 million, and the annual compound growth rate is estimated to be 1.3%. Predict the country's population in:

a) 4 years' time

b) 20 years' time.

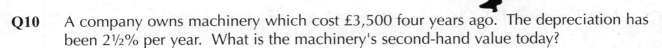

"**Appreciate**" and "**depreciate**" just mean "**increase in value**" and "**decrease in value**" — nothing more complicated than that.

Standard Index Form

Writing very big (or very small) numbers gets a bit messy with all those zeros if you don't use this standard index form. But of course, the main reason for knowing about standard form is...you guessed it — it's in the Exam.

Q1 Write as ordinary numbers:

a) 3.56×10

b) 3.56×10^3

c) 3.56×10^{-1}

d) 3.56×10^4

e) 0.082×10^2

f) 0.082×10^{-2}

g) 0.082×10

h) 0.082×10^{-1}

i) 157×10

j) 157×10^{-3}

k) 157×10^3

l) 157×10^{-1}.

Q2 Write in standard form:

a) 2.56

b) 25.6

c) 0.256

d) 25 600

e) 95.2

f) 0.0952

g) 95 200

h) 0.000952

i) 4200

j) 0.0042

k) 42

l) 420.

Q3 Write in standard form:

a) 34.7×10

b) 73.004

c) 0.005×10^3

d) 9183×10^2

e) 15 million

f) 937.1×10^4

g) 0.000075

h) 0.05×10^{-2}

i) 534×10^{-2}

j) 621.03

k) 149×10^2

l) 0.003×10^{-4} .

Write the numbers in Questions 4 to 7 in standard form.

Q4 The distance between Paris and Rome is 1476 km.

Q5 A billion = a million million   A trillion = a million million million.

Q6 A light year is 9,460,000,000,000 km (approx).

Q7 Nautilus covered 69,138 miles before having to refuel.

Q8 A rectangular field is 24,700 cm by 15,000 cm.
What is its perimeter in m? Give your answer in standard form.

Q9 This table gives the diameter and distance from the Sun of some planets.

Planet	Distance from Sun (km)	Diameter (km)
Earth	1.5×10^8	1.3×10^4
Venus	1.085×10^8	1.2×10^4
Mars	2.28×10^8	6.8×10^3
Mercury	5.81×10^7	4.9×10^3
Jupiter	7.8×10^8	1.4×10^5
Neptune	4.52×10^9	4.9×10^4
Saturn	1.43×10^9	1.2×10^5

From the table write down which planet is:

a) smallest in diameter

b) largest in diameter

c) nearest to the Sun

d) furthest from the Sun.

Write down which planets are:

e) nearer to the Sun than the Earth

f) bigger in diameter than the Earth.

Powers (Indices)

Hang on there. Before you try this page, make sure you know the seven rules for powers — you'll find them on P.20 of The Revision Guide, or you could just ask Teach.

The small number is called the <u>power</u> or <u>index number</u>. Remember the plural of index is <u>indices</u>.

$$5^4 = 5 \times 5 \times 5 \times 5 = \underline{\hspace{1cm}}$$

we say "five to the power four"

$$8^3 = 8 \times 8 \times 8 = \underline{\hspace{1cm}}$$

we say "eight to the power three" or "eight cubed"

To save time try using the power button on your calculator [x^y] [y^x]

eg. [5] [x^y] [4] [=]

[8] [x^y] [3] [=]

Q1 Complete the following:
a) $2^4 = 2 \times 2 \times 2 \times 2 =$
b) $10^3 = 10 \times 10 \times 10 =$
c) $3^5 = 3 \times ...$ $=$
d) $4^6 = 4 \times$ $=$
e) $1^9 = 1 \times$ $=$
f) $5^6 = 5 \times$ $=$

Q2 Simplify the following:
a) $2 \times 2 \times 2 \times 2 \times 2 \times 2 \times 2 \times 2$
b) $12 \times 12 \times 12 \times 12 \times 12$
c) $x \times x \times x \times x \times x \times x$
d) $m \times m \times m$
e) $y \times y \times y \times y$
f) $z \times z \times z \times z \times z \times z$

Q3 Complete the following (the first one has been done for you):
a) $10^2 \times 10^3 = (10 \times 10) \times (10 \times 10 \times 10) = 10^5$
b) $10^3 \times 10^4 =$ $=$
c) $10^4 \times 10^2 =$ $=$
d) $10^5 \times 10^3 =$ $=$
e) What is the <u>quick method</u> for writing down the final result in **b)**, **c)** and **d)**?

Easy — you'll have learnt this from your seven rules of powers.

Q4 Complete (the first one has been done for you):

a) $2^4 \div 2^2 = \dfrac{(2 \times 2 \times 2 \times 2)}{(2 \times 2)} = 2^2$

c) $4^5 \div 4^3 = \dfrac{(4 \times 4 \times 4 \times 4 \times 4)}{} =$

b) $2^5 \div 2^2 = \dfrac{(2 \times 2 \times 2 \times 2 \times 2)}{(2 \times 2)} =$

d) $8^5 \div 8^2 =$ $=$

e) What is the quick method for writing down the final result in **b)**, **c)** and **d)**?

Q5 Which of the following are <u>true</u>?

a) $2^4 \times 2^6 = 2^{10}$
b) $2^2 \times 2^3 \times 2^4 = 2^9$
c) $2^3 \times 2^2 = 2^6$

d) $4^{10} \times 4^4 \times 4^2 = 4^{18}$
e) $2^1 \times 2^3 \times 2^4 = 2^8$
f) $10^4 \times 10^2 = 10^8$

g) $2^{20} \div 2^5 = 2^4$
h) $3^{12} \div 3^4 = 3^8$
i) $4^6 \div 6^4 = 4^2$

j) $10^{20} \div 10^3 = 10^{17}$
k) $4^6 \div (4^2 \times 4^3) = 4^1$
l) $9^2 \times (9^{30} \div 9^{25}) = 9^{10}$

Q6 Remove the brackets from the following and express as a single power:
a) $(3^4 \times 3^2) \div (3^6 \times 3^3)$
b) $(4^{10} \times 4^{12}) \times 4^3$
c) $10^2 \div (10^3 \times 10^{12})$
d) $(3^6)^{-2}$
e) $4^2 \times 4^{-1} \times 4^6 \times (4^2 \div 4^3)$
f) $(5^2 \times 5^3) \div (5^6 \div 5^4)$

Basic Algebra

Q1 Work out the following temperature changes:

a) 20°C to −7°C   c) −17°C to −5°C   e) −31°C to −16°C

b) −10°C to −32°C   d) −3°C to 15°C   f) −5°C to −17°C

Q2 Which is larger and by how much?

a) −12 + 7 − 4 + 6 − 2 + 7 or b) −30 + 26 − 3 − 7 + 17

Q3 Simplify: a) $4x - 5x + 3x - x + 2x - 7x$ b) $30y - 10y + 2y - 3y + 4y - 5y$

Q4 Find the value of xy and $\dfrac{x}{y}$ for each of the following:

a) $x = -100$ $y = 10$ c) $x = -48$ $y = -3$

b) $x = 24$ $y = -4$ d) $x = 0$ $y = -4$

Q5 Find the value of $(a - b) \div (c + d)$ when $a = 10$, $b = -26$, $c = -5$ and $d = -4$.

Q6 Simplify the following:

a) $2x \times -3y$ d) $4p \times -4p$ g) $10x \div -2y$ j) $70x^2 \div -7x^2$

b) $-8a \times 2b$ e) $-30x \div -3y$ h) $-30x \div -10x$ k) $-36x^2 \div -9x$

c) $-4x \times -2x$ f) $50x \div -5y$ i) $40ab \div -10ab$ l) $40y^2 \div -5y$

Q7 Simplify the following by collecting like terms together:

a) $3x^2 + 4x + 12x^2 - 5x$ f) $15ab - 10a + b - 7a + 2ba$

b) $14x^2 - 10x - x^2 + 5x$ g) $4pq - 14p - 8q + p - q + 8p$

c) $12 - 4x^2 + 10x - 3x^2 + 2x$ h) $13x^2 + 4x^2 - 5y^2 + y^2 - x^2$

d) $20abc + 12ab + 10bac + 4b$ i) $11ab + 2cd - ba - 13dc + abc$

e) $8pq + 7p + q + 10qp - q + p$ j) $3x^2 + 4xy + 2y^2 - z^2 + 2xy - y^2 - 5x^2$

Q8 Multiply out the brackets and simplify where possible:

a) $4(x + y - z)$ h) $14(2m - n) + 2(3n - 6m)$ o) $x^2(x + 1)$

b) $x(x + 5)$ i) $4x(x + 2) - 2x(3 - x)$

c) $-3(x - 2)$ j) $3(2 + ab) + 5(1 - ab)$ p) $4x^2\left(x + 2 + \dfrac{1}{x}\right)$

d) $7(a + b) + 2(a + b)$ k) $(x - 2y)z - 2x(x + z)$ q) $8ab(a + 3 + b)$

e) $3(a + 2b) - 2(2a + b)$ l) $4(x - 2y) - (5 + x - 2y)$

f) $4(x - 2) - 2(x - 1)$ m) $a - 4(a + b)$ r) $7pq\left(p + q - \dfrac{1}{p}\right)$

g) $4e(e + 2f) + 2f(e - f)$ n) $4pq(2 + r) + 5qr(2p + 7)$ s) $4[(x + y) - 3(y - x)]$

Q9 For each of the large rectangles below, write down the area of each of the small rectangles and hence find an expression for the area of each large rectangle.

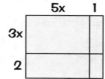

Eeeek — loads of questions...

Q10 All the expressions below have a^2 as a common factor. Factorise each of them.

a) $a^2b + a^2c$ d) $a^3 + a^2y$

b) $5a^2 + 13a^2b$ e) $2a^2x + 3a^2y + 4a^2z$

c) $2a^2b + 3a^2c$ f) $a^2b^2 + a^3c^2$

Solving Equations

Q1 When 1 is added to a number and the answer then trebled, it gives the same result as doubling the number and then adding 4. Find the number.

Q2 Solve the following:

a) $2x^2 = 18$ **b)** $2x^2 = 72$ **c)** $3x^2 = 27$ **d)** $4x^2 = 36$ **e)** $5x^2 = 5$

Q3 Solve the following:

a) $3x + 1 = 2x + 6$ **c)** $5x - 1 = 3x + 19$ **e)** $x + 15 = 4x$

b) $4x + 3 = 3x + 7$ **d)** $x + 2 = \frac{1}{2}x - 1$ **f)** $3x + 3 = 2x + 12$

Q4

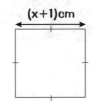

(x+1)cm

A square has sides of length $(x + 1)$ cm. Find the value of x if:

a) the perimeter of the square is 66 cm

b) the perimeter of the square is 152.8 cm.

Q5 Solve the following:

a) $3x - 8 = 7$ **d)** $2x - 9 = 25$ **f)** $5x - 2 = 6x - 7$

b) $2(x - 3) = -2$

c) $4(2x - 1) = 60$ **e)** $\frac{24}{x} + 2 = 6$ **g)** $30 - \frac{x^2}{2} = 28$

Q6 Mary is y years old. Her father is 4 times older than Mary. Her mother is 7 years younger than her father. If their three ages add up to 101 years, find the value of y. Find the ages of Mary's parents.

Q7 Mr Smith sent his car to the local garage. He spent £x on new parts, four times this amount on labour and finally £29 for an MOT test. If the total bill was for £106.50, find the value of x.

Q8 Solve:

a) $2(x - 3) - (x - 2) = 5$ **g)** $\frac{x}{3} + 7 = 12$ **j)** $41 - \frac{x}{11} = 35$

b) $5(x + 2) - 3(x - 5) = 29$

c) $2(x + 2) + 3(x + 4) = 31$ **h)** $\frac{x}{10} + 18 = 29$ **k)** $\frac{x}{100} - 3 = 4$

d) $10(x + 3) - 4(x - 2) = 7(x + 5)$

e) $5(4x + 3) = 4(7x - 5) + 3(9 - 2x)$ **i)** $17 - \frac{x^2}{3} = 5$ **l)** $\frac{120}{x} = 16$

f) $3(7 + 2x) + 2(1 - x) = 19$

Q9 Joan, Kate and Linda win £2,400 on the National Lottery between them. Joan gets a share of £x, whilst Kate gets twice as much as Joan. Linda's share is £232 less than Joan's amount.

a) Write down an expression for the amounts Joan, Kate and Linda win.

b) Write down an expression in terms of x, and solve it.

c) Write down the amounts Kate and Linda receive.

Q10 All the angles in the diagram are right angles.

a) Write down an expression for the perimeter of the shape.

b) Write down an expression for the area of the shape.

c) For what value of x will the perimeter and area be numerically equal?

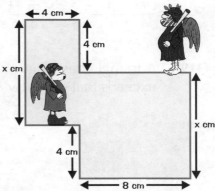

Big blobs and broomsticks...

Solving Equations

Q11   Solve the following:

a) $5(x - 1) + 3(x - 4) = -11$

b) $3(x + 2) + 2(x - 4) = x - 3(x + 3)$

c) $\dfrac{3x}{2} + 3 = x$

d) $3(4x + 2) = 2(2x - 1)$

e) $\dfrac{5x + 7}{9} = 3$

f) $\dfrac{2x + 7}{11} = 3$

Q12   Two men are decorating a room. One has painted 20 m² and the other only 6 m². They continue painting and manage to paint another x m² each. If the first man has painted exactly three times the area painted by the second man, find the value of x.

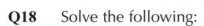

It's easy — you just put the 2 bits together and there's your equation. Then all you've got to do is solve it...

Q13   For what value of x is the expression $14 - \dfrac{x}{2}$ equal to the value $\dfrac{3x - 4}{2}$?

Q14   Carol's father was 24 years old when Carol was born. Now he is four times as old as Carol. How old is Carol?

Q15   Mr Jones is 4 years older than his wife and 31 years older than his son. Their ages add up to 82 years. If Mr Jones is x years old, find the value of x and find the age of his wife and son.

Q16   Solve the following:

a) $\dfrac{y}{2} + 2 = 13$

b) $\dfrac{3x}{4} - 2 = 4$

c) $\dfrac{2z}{5} - 3 = -5$

d) $\dfrac{1}{5}(x - 4) = 3$

e) $\dfrac{2}{3}(x + 1) = 16$

f) $\dfrac{3}{5}(4x - 3) = 15$

g) $\dfrac{8}{x^2} = \dfrac{32}{36}$

h) $\dfrac{12}{5x^2} = \dfrac{3}{20}$

i) $\dfrac{14}{3x^2} = \dfrac{2}{21}$

Q17   A train travels at 70 mph for x hours and then at 80 mph for $3\frac{3}{4}$ hours. If the train covers 405 miles of track, find the value of x.

Q18   Solve the following:

a) $\dfrac{4x + 3}{2} + x = \dfrac{5x + 41}{4}$

b) $\dfrac{5}{7}(x - 2) - \dfrac{3}{4}(x + 3) = -4$

Q19   A triangle has lengths as shown below. Find the length of each side, if the length of AC exceeds that of AB by ½ cm.

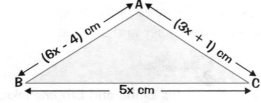

Trial and Improvement

Q1 The cubic equation $x^3 + x = 24$ has a solution between 2 and 3.
Copy the table below and use it to find this solution to 1 d.p.

Guess(x)	Value of $x^3 + x$	Too large or Too small
2	$2^3 + 2 =$	
3	$3^3 + 3 =$	

Q2 The cubic equation $x^3 - x^2 + x = 7$ has a solution between 2 and 3.
Copy the table below and use it to find this solution to 1 d.p.

Guess(x)	Value of $x^3 - x^2 + x$	Too large or Too small
2	$(2)^3 - (2)^2 + (2) =$	
3	$(3)^3 - (3)^2 + (3) =$	

Q3 The cubic equation $x^3 - x^2 = 0.7$ has a solution between 1 and 2.
Copy the table on the right and use it to find this solution to 1 d.p.

Guess(x)	Value of $x^3 - x^2$	Too large or Too small
1	$(1)^3 - (1)^2 =$	
2	$(2)^3 - (2)^2 =$	

Q4 The cubic equation $x^3 + x^2 - 4x = 3$ has three solutions. The first solution lies between –3 and –2. The second lies between –1 and 0. The third solution lies between 1 and 2.
Copy the table below and use it to find all three solutions.

Guess(x)	Value of $x^3 + x^2 - 4x$	Too large or Too small
–3	$(-3)^3 + (-3)^2 - 4(-3) = -6$	
–2	$(-2)^3 + (-2)^2 - 4(-2) =$	
–1	$(-1)^3 + (-1)^2 - 4(-1) =$	
0	$(0)^3 + (0)^2 - 4(0) =$	
1	$(1)^3 + (1)^2 - 4(1) =$	
2	$(2)^3 + (2)^2 - 4(2) =$	

The first solution is .... to 1d.p.

The second solution is .... to 1d.p.

The third solution is .... to 1d.p.

They don't always give you the starting numbers — so if they don't, make sure you pick two opposite cases (one too big, one too small), or you've blown it.

STAGE ONE

Sequences

Q1   10, 20, 15, 17½, 16¼...
     a) Write down the next 4 terms.
     b) Explain how you would work out the 10th term.

Q2   Write down the nth term:
     a) 1, 4, 9, 16, 25...
     b) 3, 6, 11, 18, 27...
     c) 1, 8, 27, 64, 125...
     d) ½, 4, 13½, 32, 62½...

Q3   Calculate the 100th term:
     a) 1, 4, 9, 16 ...
     b) 1, $\sqrt{2}$, $\sqrt{3}$, $\sqrt{4}$ ...
     c) $\sqrt{3}$, 2, $\sqrt{5}$, $\sqrt{6}$ ...
     d) $\sqrt{2}$, $\sqrt{4}$, $\sqrt{6}$, $\sqrt{8}$, $\sqrt{10}$ ...

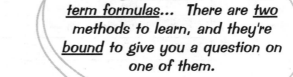

You've <u>got to know</u> those <u>nth term formulas</u>... There are <u>two</u> methods to learn, and they're <u>bound</u> to give you a question on one of them.

Q4   Sequence A   1, 4, 9, 16, 25,...
        Sequence B   3, 6, 9, 12, 15,...
        Sequence C   2, 5, 9, 14, 20,...

     a) Write down the next three terms in sequence A.
     b) Write down the next three terms in sequence B.
     c) Write down the nth term of sequence A.
     d) Write down the nth term of sequence B.
     e) Sequence C is obtained from sequences A and B. Using this information and your answers to parts **c)** and **d)** work out the nth term for sequence C.

Q5   Jimmy uses some stones to make a pattern.

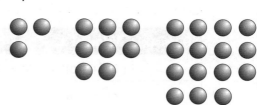

     a) How many stones will there be in the next block?
     b) How many stones will there be in the nth block?
     c) There are 2600 stones in a block. Use your answer to **b)** to find the corresponding value for n.

Q6   The first term of a certain sequence is 1. The second term of the sequence is also 1. The nth term is found using the following formula:
        nth term = $(n-1)$th term + $(n-2)$th term.
    Calculate the third, fourth, and fifth terms in the sequence.

Q7   In order to work out the evaporation rate, Joanna measured the area of a puddle of water every hour on the hour. At 1300h the area of the puddle was 128 cm². 1 hour later the area of the puddle was 64 cm². At 1500h the area was 32 cm².

     a) What was the area of the puddle of water at 1600h?
     b) What was the area of the puddle at 1800h?

Sequences

Q8   In the following sequences, write down the next 3 terms and the nth term:

a) 7, 10, 13, 16,...
c) 6, 16, 26, 36,...
b) 12, 17, 22, 27,...
d) 54, 61, 68, 75,...

Q9   The first four terms of a sequence are x, $4x$, $9x$, $16x$.

a) For $x = 2$ write down the next two terms in the sequence.
b) For $x = 2$ write down the nth term in the sequence.
c) For $x = 3$ write down the nth term in the sequence.
d) Write down the nth term, valid for any value of x.

Q10   Calculate the 34th term in the following sequences:

a) $1, \dfrac{1}{2}, \dfrac{1}{3}, \dfrac{1}{4} \dots$

b) 10, 20, 30, 40...

c) 0, 3, 8, 15, 24...

d) $1, x, x^2, x^3, x^4 \dots$

Q11

  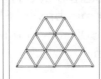

The pattern above is based on individual triangles.

a) Write down the number of triangles in each group.
b) Work out the number of triangles that would be in each of the next three groups.
c) Find a formula for the number of triangles in the nth term of the pattern.

Q12   A square tile pattern is formed with grey and white tiles. In the centre there is always a grey tile. The rest of the pattern is made up of alternating grey and white tiles, with the four corner tiles of the square always being grey.
Assume that $n = 1$ in the pattern shown opposite.

Work out, in terms of n, the formula for:

a) the number of grey tiles
b) the number of white tiles
c) the total number of tiles.

Q13   Write down the next three terms and nth term of:

a) 5, 8, 12, 17,...
b) 6, 9, 14, 21,...
c) 9, 12, 19, 30,...
d) 14, 19, 27, 38,...

e) 729, 243, 81, 27,...
f) 31 250, 6250, 1250, 250,...
g) 12 288, 3072, 768, 192,...
h) 5103, 1701, 567, 189,...

If the difference between terms is always decreasing, there's going to be a limit to the sequence.

D/T Graphs and V/T Graphs

Q1 This diagram shows the different times taken by 5 trains to travel 100 km.

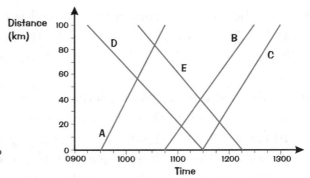

a) Calculate the speed of each train.

b) How could you tell by looking at the diagram which was the fastest and which the slowest?

c) Train D should have been travelling at 50 km/hr. How many minutes late was it?

Q2 Two cars start a journey at midday (1200) — one from town A and the other from village B. A and B are 80 km apart. The car from town A travels at an average speed of 48 km/hr and the other car, from village B, at 60 km/hr.

a) Draw a graph to show these journeys.

b) At what time do the cars pass? (approx.)

c) How far from A are they when they pass?

Q3 A girl set off on an all-day walk. She started at 0915 and walked at a steady speed for 9 km before stopping at 1100 for a 20 min break. She then set off again at a steady speed and walked 8 km, stopping at 1300 for 45 mins. After lunch she walked at 3½ km/hr for 2½ hrs to her destination.

a) Draw a graph to show this walk.

b) How far did she walk altogether?

c) What was the average speed for the whole walk?

d) What was her fastest walking speed?

You need to remember what the different bits of a travel graph mean — what it looks like when <u>stopped</u>, <u>changing speed</u> and <u>coming back</u> to the starting point.

Q4 On sports day the first three in the 1000 m race ran as shown.

a) Which runner, A, B or C, won the race?

b) How long did the winner take?

c) Which runner kept up a steady speed?

d) What was that speed
   i) in m/min?
   ii) km/hr?

e) Which runner achieved the fastest speed and what was that speed?

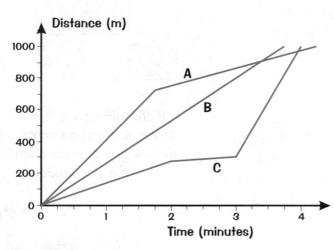

Plotting Straight Lines

Q1 Complete the following table for the line $y = 3x - 1$:

x	-4	-3	-2	-1	0	1	2	3	4
3x									
-1									
y									

Plot these points on graph paper and hence draw the graph of $y = 3x - 1$. Use a scale of 1 cm for 2 units on the y-axis and 2 cm for 1 unit on the x-axis.

Q2 Complete the following table for the line $y = \frac{1}{2}x - 3$:

x	-6	-4	-2	0	2	4	6
½ x							
-3							
y							

Plot these points on graph paper and hence draw the graph of $y = \frac{1}{2}x - 3$.

Q3 Complete the following table for the line $y = -\frac{x}{4} - 2$.

Plot these points on graph paper and draw the graph of $y = -\frac{x}{4} - 2$.

x	-12	-6	6
y			

Use your graph to find:
    a) The value of y when $x = -4$
    b) The value of y when $x = -1$
    c) The value of x when $y = -2.75$
    d) The value of x when $y = 0$

Q4 The cost of hiring a car is calculated using the formula:
Total cost = £25 + 20p for each kilometre travelled.
Copy and complete this table:

Number of kilometres	0	50	100	200	300	350
Total cost in £						

Plot these points on a graph (put distance travelled on the horizontal axis and total cost on the vertical axis). Use your graph to find the cost of hiring the car when the following distances have been travelled:
a) 170 km   **b)** 270 km   **c)** 320 km

Use your graph to find the number of kilometres travelled when this total cost is:
d) £78   **e)** £34   **f)** £42

Plotting Straight Lines & Curves

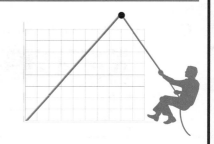

Q1 The cost of electricity is calculated using the formula:
Total cost = Fixed charge + cost per unit.

Customers can choose two different methods of payment:
Method A: Fixed charge £10, cost per unit 25p
Method B: Fixed charge £40, cost per unit 5p
Copy and complete this table:

Number of Units used	0	100	200	300
Cost using method A				
Cost using method B				

Plot these points on a graph (put the number of units on the horizontal axis, cost on the vertical axis).

a) Use your graph to find the total cost when 70 units are used for:
  i) Method A
  ii) Method B

b) Miss Wright used 75 units. Which method should she use to minimise her bill, Method A or Method B?

c) Mr Jones and Mrs Green both used exactly the same number of units and paid the same amount. Mr Jones used Method A, while Mrs Green used Method B. How many units did they each use?

 In case you hadn't noticed, it's always a good idea to put *lots of steps* in the *table of values* — that way it's *easier to check* any points that look wrong.

Q2 Complete this table of values for $y = x^2 + 2$:

x	-3	-2	-1	0	1	2	3
x^2							
+2							
y							

Draw the graph of $y = x^2 + 2$

Q3 Complete this table of values for $y = 2x^2 - 4$:

x	-3	-2	-1	0	1	2	3
$2x^2$							
-4							
y							

Draw the graph of $y = 2x^2 - 4$

Q4 Complete this table of values for $y = -x^2 + 2$:

x	-3	-2	-1	0	1	2	3
$-x^2$							
+2							
y							

Draw the graph of $y = -x^2 + 2$

Q5 Complete this table of values for $y = -2x^2 + 6$:

x	-3	-2	-1	0	1	2	3
$-2x^2$							
+6							
y							

Draw the graph of $y = -2x^2 + 6$

Pythagoras and Bearings

Don't try and do it all in your head — you've got to label the sides or you're bound to mess it up. Go on, get your pen out...

Q1 Find the unknown length in each of the following triangles.

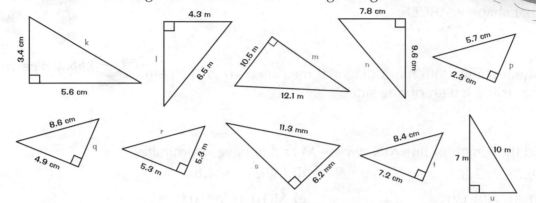

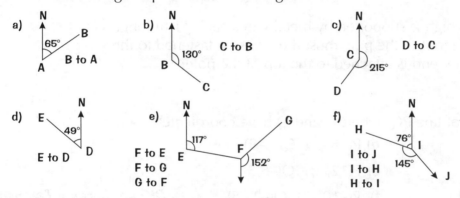

It's easy to get lost if you don't follow the easy rules: always measure bearings from the __North Line__ and always measure __Clockwise__.

Q2 Find the bearings required in these diagrams.

a) N 65° B
   A B to A

b) N 130° C to B
   B
   C

c) N
   C D to C
   215°
   D

d) E 49° N
   E to D D

e) N 117° G
   F to E E F
   F to G 152°
   G to F

f) N
   H 76° I
   I to J 145°
   I to H J
   H to I

Q3 A walker travels 1200 m on a bearing of 165° and then another 1500 m on a bearing of 210°. By accurate measurement find how far she is now from her starting point. What bearing must she walk on to return to base?

Q4 A plane flies due east for 153 km then turns and flies due north for 116 km. How far is it now from where it started?

Q5 A coastguard spots a boat on a bearing of 040° and at a distance of 350 m. He can also see a tree due east of him. If the tree is due south of the boat, draw a diagram and measure accurately the distances of the:

a) boat to the tree

b) coastguard to the tree.

c) Check by Pythagoras to see if your answers are reasonable.

Q6 a) Calculate the lengths WY and ZY.
   b) What is the total distance WXYZW?
   c) What is the area of quadrilateral WXYZ?

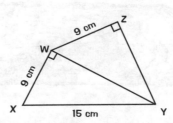

Pythagoras and Coordinates

Q1   The coordinates of four points are A(2,1), B(6,4), C(7,0)
and D(3,–3). Calculate the distances:

a) AB   **b)** BC   **c)** CD   **d)** BD   **e)** AC

f) What shape is ABCD?

ahh... nice 'n' easy...

Q2   A square tablecloth has a diagonal measurement of 130 cm.
What is the length of one side?

Q3   Find the length of line MN, where M and N have coordinates:

a) M(6,3) N(2,8)   **d)** M(9,5) N(4,8)

b) M(1,5) N(8,12)   **e)** M(10,4) N(10,0)

c) M(0,1) N(7,3)   **f)** M(12,6) N(13,0)

Q4   A flagpole 10 m high is supported by metal wires each 11 m long.
How far from the foot of the pole must the wires be fastened to the
ground if the other end is attached to the top of the pole?

Q5   Find the length of line PQ, where P and Q have coordinates:

a) P(2,–3) Q(3,0)   **d)** P(–6,–1) Q(7,–9)

b) P(1,–8) Q(4,3)   **e)** P(12,–3) Q(–5,5)

c) P(0,–1) Q(2,–3)   **f)** P(–10,–2) Q(–2,–8)

*OK, so there's a few negative
numbers creeping in here, but
they're really no harder.*

Q6   Find the length of each of the lines on
this graph.

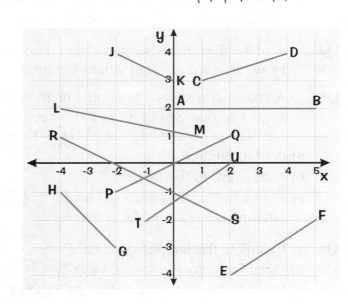

Trigonometry

Q1 Calculate the tan, sin and cos of each of these angles:
a) 17°　　**b)** 83°　　**c)** 5°　　**d)** 28°　　**e)** 45°.

Before you start a trigonometry question, write down the ratios, using
SOH CAH TOA (Sockatoa!) — *it'll help you pick your formula triangle.*

Q2 Use the tangent ratio to find the unknowns:

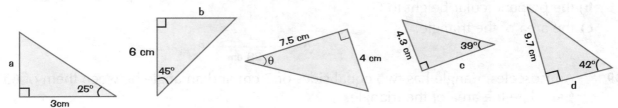

Q3 Use the cosine ratio to find the unknowns:

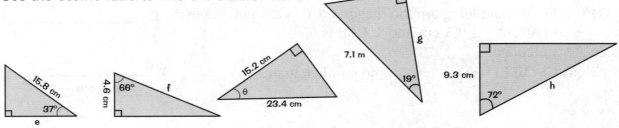

Q4 Use the sine ratio to find the unknowns:

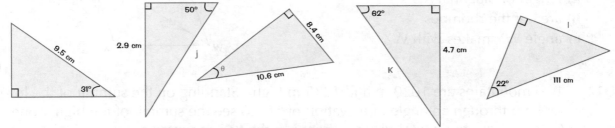

Q5 Find the unknowns using the appropriate ratios:

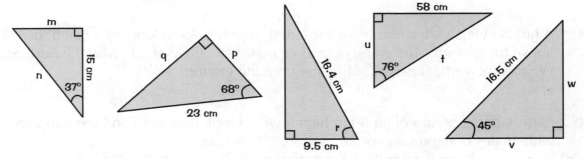

Q6 Calculate the height of the tree using the measurements in the diagram.

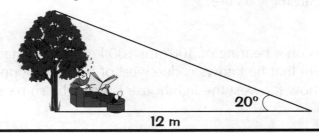

Trigonometry

Q7 A boat travels 9 km due south and then 7 km due east. What bearing must it travel on to return to base?

Make sure you've got the hang of the <u>inverse</u> SIN, COS and TAN functions on your calc... and check it's in <u>DEG</u> mode or you'll get nowhere fast.

Q8 This isosceles triangle has a base of 28 cm and a top angle of 54°. Calculate:

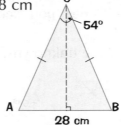

a) the length of sides AC and BC
b) the perpendicular height to C
c) the area of the triangle.

Q9 An isosceles triangle has two equal sides of 7 cm and an angle between them of 65°. Calculate the area of the triangle.

Q10 In this parallelogram the diagonal CB is at right angles to AC. AB is 9.5 cm and ∠CAB is 60°. Calculate:

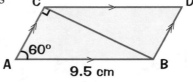

a) CB b) BD c) the area of the parallelogram.

Q11 This rhombus WXYZ has base 15 cm and diagonal WY of 28 cm. Calculate the:

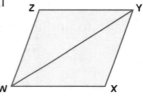

a) length of diagonal XZ
b) area of the rhombus
c) angle WY makes with WX.

Q12 Two mountains are 1020 m and 1235 m high. Standing on the summit of the lower one I look up through an angle of elevation of 16° to see the summit of the higher one. Calculate the horizontal distance between the two mountains.

Q13 A girl is flying a kite. She holds the string, which is 45 m long, at a height of 1.3 m above the ground. The string of the kite makes an angle of 33° with the horizontal. What is the vertical height of the kite from the ground?

Q14 I am standing on top of an 80 m high tower. I look due north and see two cars with angles of depression of 38° and 49°. Calculate:
a) how far each car is from the base of the tower
b) how far apart the cars are.

Q15 A ship sails on a bearing of 300° for 100 km. The captain can then see a lighthouse due south of him that he knows is due west of his starting point. Calculate how far west the lighthouse is from the ship's starting point.

Similarity and Enlargement

Q1 The side view of a playground swing is shown in the diagram. Triangles PQR and PST are similar.

a) Write down the distance PT.

b) Calculate the distance ST.

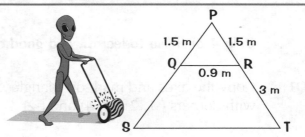

Q2 A box of chocolates is to have the shape of a cuboid 15 cm long, 8 cm wide and 10 cm high.

a) Calculate the area of material needed to make the box (assuming no flaps are required for glueing).

b) In advertising the chocolates, the manufacturer decides he will have a box made in a similar shape. The enlargement is to have a scale factor of 50. Calculate the area of material required to make the box for publicity. Give your answer in square metres.

Q3

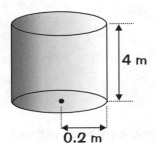

A scale model of a proposed water tower is as shown. The model is a cylinder of height 4 m and base radius 0.2 m. The proposed height of the full size tower is 1000 m.

a) What is the base radius of the full size tower?

b) Calculate, in cubic metres, the volume of the scale model.

c) How many times larger than the scale model is the volume of the proposed water tower?

Q4 Draw accurately and label:

a) the image $A_1B_1C_1$ of the triangle ABC after an enlargement scale factor 2 about the point 0

b) the image $A_2B_2C_2$ of the triangle ABC after an enlargement scale factor –1 about the point 0.

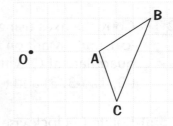

Q5 On a holiday near the sea, children built a sandcastle in the shape of a cone. The radius of the base is 100 cm and the height is 100 cm.

a) What is the volume of the sandcastle in m³ correct to 3 significant figures?
The children now remove the top portion to make a similar cone but only 50 cm in height.

b) State the radius of the base of this smaller cone.

c) State the ratio of the volume of the small cone to the volume of the original cone.

d) Calculate the volume of the small cone in m³ correct to 3 significant figures.

e) Write down the ratio of the volume of the portion left of the original cone to the smaller cone in the form *n*:1.

The Four Transformations

Only 4 of these to learn... and good old TERRY's always around to help if you need him.

Q1 Copy the axes and mark on triangle A with corners (-1, 2), (0, 4) and (-2, 4).

Use a scale of 1 cm to 1 unit.

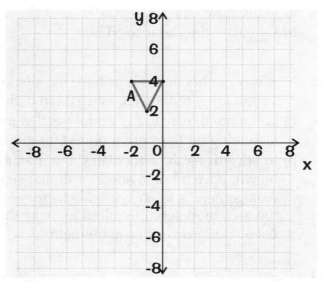

a) Reflect A in the line $y = -x$.
Label this image B.
b) Reflect A in the line $x = 1$.
Label the image C.
c) Reflect A in the line $y = -1$.
Label the image D.
d) Translate triangle D with the
vector $\begin{pmatrix} 4 \\ 2 \end{pmatrix}$. Label this image E.
e) Translate triangle C with the vector $\begin{pmatrix} 3 \\ -3 \end{pmatrix}$. Label this image F.
f) Describe fully the transformation that sends C to E.
g) Describe fully the transformation that sends F to A.

 Transformations... just about the most fun you can have without crying.

Q2 Copy the axes using a scale of 1 cm to 1 unit. Mark on the axes a quadrilateral Q with corners (-2, 1), (-3, 1), (-3, 3) and (-2, 3).

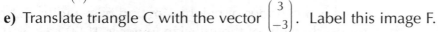

a) Rotate Q clockwise through 90° about the point (-1, 2). Label the image R.
b) Rotate R clockwise through 90° about the point (0, 1). Label the image S.
c) Describe fully the rotation that maps Q to S.
d) Describe fully the translation that sends Q to S.
e) Describe fully the reflection that sends Q to S.
f) Rotate Q through 180° about the point (-½, -1). Label the image T.
g) Rotate Q anticlockwise through 90° about the point (-1, -1). Label the image U.
h) Describe fully the rotation that sends U to T.

The Four Transformations

 Move each point separately — then check your shape hasn't done anything unexpected while you weren't looking.

Q3 Copy the axes below using a scale of 1 cm to 1 unit.

A parallelogram A has vertices at (6, 4), (10, 4), (8, 10) and (12, 10). Draw this parallelogram onto your axes. An enlargement scale factor ½ and centre (0,0) transforms parallelogram A onto its image B.

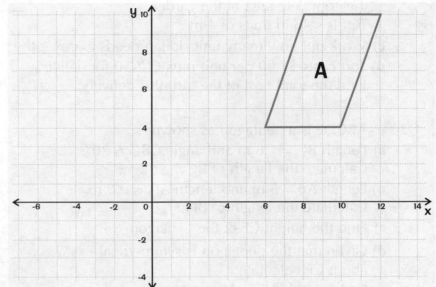

a) Draw this image B on your axes.

b) Translate B by the vector $\begin{pmatrix} -3 \\ -2 \end{pmatrix}$ and label this image C.

c) Calculate the ratio of the area of parallelogram C to the area of parallelogram A.

Q4 Draw axes with x and y running from 0 to 12 with a scale of 1 cm to 1 unit.

O is the origin. $\overrightarrow{OP} = \begin{pmatrix} 4 \\ 2 \end{pmatrix}$, $\overrightarrow{PQ} = \begin{pmatrix} -1 \\ 2 \end{pmatrix}$, and $\overrightarrow{QR} = 2\,\overrightarrow{OP}$.

a) Mark P, Q and R on your axes.

b) Calculate the lengths of the vectors $\overrightarrow{OP}$ and $\overrightarrow{OQ}$.

c) Find the equation of the line joining P and Q.

d) Give R the translation $\overrightarrow{QO}$. Label the image T.

e) Verify that $\overrightarrow{PQ} + \overrightarrow{QR} + \overrightarrow{RT} + \overrightarrow{TP} = O$.

Urghh — **vectors**...
Make sure you get the coordinates the right way round — **top** for **x** dir^n, **bottom** for **y** dir^n.

Q5 In the diagram, A is the point (4, 3), B is (4, 1) and C is (5, 1).

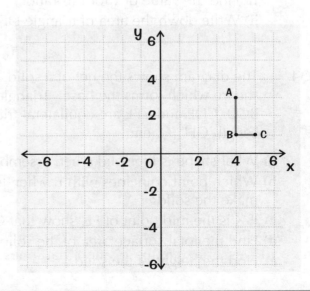

a) Using a scale of 1cm to 1 unit draw the diagram and mark on it the figure given by ABC.

b) Reflect ABC in the x-axis and label the image $A_1B_1C_1$.

c) Reflect $A_1B_1C_1$ in the y-axis and label the image $A_2B_2C_2$.

d) Describe fully the single transformation which would map ABC onto $A_2B_2C_2$.

Areas

Q1 The diagram shows a plan of Julian's garden.

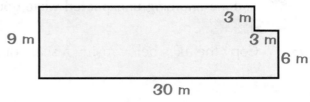

a) Calculate the perimeter of the garden.

b) Find the area of the garden.

Julian wishes to buy turf to cover
the complete area of the garden.
Turf is sold in units of 4 m².

c) Work out how many units Julian needs to cover the whole garden.

d) Turf costs £7.90 per unit plus £12.50 for delivery.
Find the total cost of the turf plus delivery.

Q2 ABCDE is a pentagon as shown.

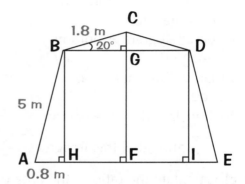

a) Length BC = 1.8 m and angle CBG = 20°.
Calculate the length of BG.

b) Length AB = 5 m and length AH = 0.8 m.
Calculate the length of BH.

c) Find the height CF of the pentagon.

d) Given that the pentagon is symmetrical
about CF calculate:

  i) the width AE of the pentagon

  ii) the area of the pentagon ABCDE.

Q3 ABCD is a field with AB = 100 m, BC = 90 m
and CD = 60 m. DE is a fence across the
field with EA = x m.

a) Find the area of the field ABCD.

b) Find an expression in terms of x for the
area of triangle DEA.

c) The fence DE is arranged so that the ratio of the area of triangle DEA : area of trapezium
BEDC = 3:5.

  i) Find the value of x for this ratio.

  ii) Write down the area of triangle DEA using the value of x found in **i)**.

Q4 The diagram shows the net of a solid. EFGH is a
square which forms the base. Triangles ABC,
BCD, CDE and CFE are equilateral triangles.
Length GH = 6 cm.

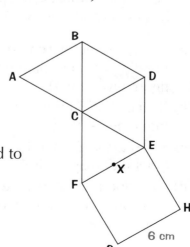

a) What shape is the solid when assembled?

b) Which point coincides with B when the net is assembled to
make the solid?

c) If X is the mid point of FE, show that CX is 5.20 cm.

d) Find the total surface area of the solid.

e) Find the height of the solid.

Volumes

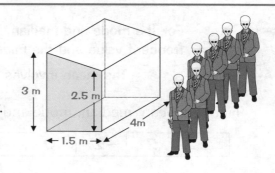

Q1 Busy Buses Ltd decide to put a bus shelter near their main town centre stop. It is a prism with the dimensions shown.

a) Find the area of the cross-section of the shelter.

b) Find its volume.

Q2

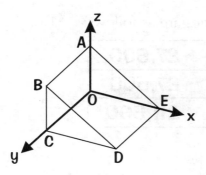

The diagram shows a triangular prism.
The coordinates of A are (0, 0, 5).
The coordinates of E are (4, 0, 0).
The coordinates of C are (0, 8, 0).

a) Write down the coordinates of:
   i) B
   ii) D.

b) Calculate the volume of the prism.

Q3 A cuboid has a height of x m, a width of $(3 - x)$ m and a length of $(5 - x)$ m.

a) Write down an expression for the volume of the cuboid.

b) Complete the table of values using your expression for the volume of the cuboid.

x	0	1	2	3
V			6	

c) Draw a graph of V against x for $0 \leqslant x \leqslant 3$.

d) Use your graph to estimate the maximum volume of the cuboid.

e) Estimate the surface area of the cuboid when the volume is at its maximum.

f) A particular cuboid has a volume of 6 m³.
By using your graph to find the two possible values of x, estimate the maximum total surface area of the cuboid for this volume.

Q4 Bill bought a new garden shed with dimensions as shown. Find:

a) the area of the cross-section

b) the volume of the shed

c) the length AB

d) the total area of the roof.

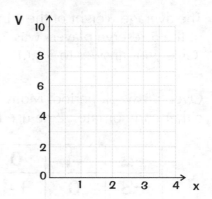

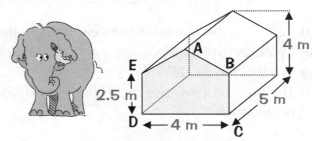

Q5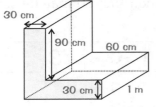

Jill buys a bookshelf with the dimensions shown in the diagram.

a) Find the cross-sectional area.

b) Find the volume of the bookshelf in m³.

Mean, Median, Mode, Range

For the mode and median, just identify the most frequent value and the middle value — easy.

The mean involves a bit more calculation, but hey, you are doing maths.

Q1 Find the mean, median, mode and range of these numbers:

1	2	−2	0	1	8	3	−3	2	4	−2	2

Q2 A small company has 9 employees. Their salaries are as follows:

£13,000	£9,000	£7,500
£18,000	£12,000	£7,500
£23,000	£15,000	£11,500

a) Find the mean, median and mode of their salaries.

b) Which one does not give a good indication of their average salary?

Q3 The mean daily weight of potatoes sold in a greengrocer's from Monday to Friday was 14 kg. The mean daily weight of potatoes sold from Monday to Saturday was 15 kg. How many kg of potatoes were sold on Saturday?

Q4 The average weight of the 11 players in a football team was 72.5 kg. The average weight of the 5 reserve players was 75.6 kg. What was the average weight of the whole squad? (Give your answer to 3 s.f.)

Q5 Over a 3-week period, Molly kept a record of how many minutes her school bus was either early or late. (She used + for late and – for early.)

+2	−1	0	+5	−4	−7	0
−8	0	+4	−4	−3	+14	+2

a) Calculate the mean lateness/earliness of the bus.

b) Calculate the median.

c) What is the mode?

d) The bus company use the answers to **a)**, **b)** and **c)** to claim they are always on time. Is this true?

Q6 The local rugby team scored the following number of tries in their first 10 matches of the season:

3	5	4	2	0	1	3	0	3	4

Find their modal number of tries.

Mean, Median, Mode, Range

Q7 Colin averaged 83% over 3 exams. His average for the first two exams was 76%. What was Colin's score in the final exam?

Q8 The bar graph shows the amount of time Jim and Bob spend watching TV during the week.

a) Find the mean amount of time per day each spends watching TV.

b) Find the range of times for each of them.

c) Using these values, comment on what you notice.

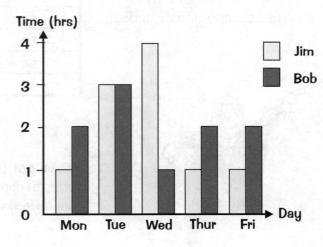

Q9 In each of the following cases, decide which average is referred to:
a) this average is least appropriate when the total number of values is small
b) this average is least affected if one of the values is removed at random
c) this average is most affected by the presence of extreme values.

Q10 Mr Jones posted 88 Christmas cards first class on Monday. His friends received them over the week: 40 on Tuesday, 28 on Wednesday, 9 on Thursday, 6 on Friday and the remainder on Saturday.

a) Find the modal number of days it took for the cards to arrive.

b) Find the median number of days it took for the cards to arrive.

c) "The majority of first class post arrives within 2 days." Is the above statement true or false in the light of the data?

Q11 The range for a certain list of numbers is 26, one of the numbers in the list is 48.
a) What is the lowest possible value a number in the list could be?
b) What is the highest possible value that could be in the list?

Q12 An ordinary dice is rolled 6 times, landing on a different number each time.
a) What is the mean score?
b) What is the median score?
c) What is the range of scores?

Frequency Tables

Q1 130 female bus drivers were weighed to the nearest kg.
Calculate:
a) the median weight
b) the modal weight
c) the mean weight, by
first completing the table.

Weight (kg)	Frequency	Weight × Frequency
51	40	
52	30	
53	45	
54	10	
55	5	

You've got to be able to do these in both row and column form, because they could give you either one. There's no real difference, and the rules are still the same.

Q2 A travel company logs all calls to their sales desk. The number of calls per day received by the sales desk over a given year are shown below.

No. of Calls	10	11	12	13	14	15	16 and over
No. of Days	110	70	120	27	18	12	8

a) Find the median number of calls.
b) Find the modal number of calls.

Q3 A student has classes in Mathematics (M), English (E), French (F), Art (A) and Science (S). Her timetable is shown opposite.

Monday	S S E E A
Tuesday	E M M A A
Wednesday	S M E F F
Thursday	F E E A S
Friday	M M E S S

a) Complete the following frequency table for a week's lessons:

b) Calculate the number of French lessons that the student will attend during a 12-week term.

Subject	M	E	F	A	S
Frequency					

c) What is the modal lesson?

Frequency Tables

Q4 20 pupils are asked to estimate the length (to the nearest m) of their gardens.
Here are the results: 10, 8, 6, 4, 10, 8, 0, 14, 12, 8, 10, 6, 1, 6, 10, 8, 6, 6, 8, 8
Copy the frequency table below and put the estimates in.

a) Find the mode of the data.
b) Find the median of the data.
c) State the range of the data.

Length (m)	4 and under	6	8	10	12	14 and over
Frequency						

Q5 Using the computerised till in a shoe shop, the manager can predict what stock to order
from the previous week's sales.
Opposite is the tabularised printout
for <u>last week</u> for <u>men's shoes</u>.

Shoe size	5	6	7	8	9	10	11
frequency	9	28	56	70	56	28	9

a) The mean, mode and median for this data can be compared. For each of the following
statements decide whether it is true or false.
  i) The <u>mode</u> for this data is <u>70</u>.
  ii) The <u>mean</u> is <u>greater than</u> the <u>median</u> for this distribution.
  iii) The mean, median and mode are <u>all equal</u> in this distribution.

b) What <u>percentage</u> of customers bought shoes of the <u>mean size</u> from last week's sales data:

  i) 30%   **ii)** 70%   **iii)** 0.273%   or   **iv)** 27.3%?

Q6 A survey is carried out in a small village to find out how many bedrooms the houses
have. The frequency table displays the results.

No. of bedrooms	1	2	3	4	5
Frequency	3	5	6	2	4

Find the mean, mode and median of the data.

Q7 A tornado has struck the hamlet of Moose-on-the-Wold. Many houses have
had windows broken. The frequency table shows the devastating effects.

No. of windows broken per house	0	1	2	3	4	5	6
Frequency	5	3	4	11	13	7	2

a) Calculate the modal number of broken windows.
b) Calculate the median number of broken windows.
c) Calculate the mean number of broken windows.

Grouped Frequency

Q1   The weights in kg of 18 newly felled trees are noted below:

272.7	333.2	251.0	246.5	328.0	259.6	200.2	312.8
344.3	226.8	362.0	348.3	256.1	232.9	309.7	398.0
284.5	327.4						

a) Complete the frequency table.

Weight (kg)	Tally	Frequency	Mid-Interval	Frequency × Mid-Interval
200 – 249				
250 – 299				
300 – 349				
350 – 399				

b) Estimate the mean weight using the frequency table.

c) What is the modal group?

Q2   The speeds of 32 skiers at a certain corner of a downhill course are tabulated below.

Speed (km/h)	40 – 44	45 – 49	50 – 54	55 – 59	60 – 64
Frequency	4	8	10	7	3
Mid-Interval					
Frequency × Mid-Interval					

a) By completing the frequency table, estimate the mean speed.

b) How many skiers were travelling at less than 54.5 km/h?

c) How many skiers were travelling at more than 49.5 km/h?

Q3   48 numbers are recorded below:

0.057	0.805	0.056	0.979	0.419	0.160	0.534	0.763
0.642	0.569	0.773	0.055	0.349	0.892	0.664	0.136
0.528	0.792	0.085	0.546	0.549	0.908	0.639	0.000
0.614	0.478	0.421	0.472	0.292	0.579	0.542	0.356
0.070	0.890	0.883	0.333	0.033	0.323	0.544	0.668
0.094	0.049	0.049	0.999	0.632	0.700	0.983	0.356

a) Transfer the data into the frequency table.

Number	$0 \leqslant n < 0.2$	$0.2 \leqslant n < 0.4$	$0.4 \leqslant n < 0.6$	$0.6 \leqslant n < 0.8$	$0.8 \leqslant n < 1$
Tally					
Frequency					
Mid-Interval					
Frequency × Mid-Interval					

b) Which is the modal class?

c) Which group contains the median?

d) Estimate the mean value.

Cumulative Frequency

Q1   Using the cumulative frequency curve, read off the:

    a) median
    b) lower quartile
    c) upper quartile
    d) interquartile range.

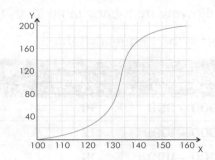

Q2   The number of passengers using a bus service each day has been recorded over a 4-week period. The data is presented in the table below:

No. passengers	0 – 49	50 – 99	100 – 149	150 – 199	200 – 249	250 – 299
Frequency	2	7	10	5	3	1
Cumulative Frequency						
Mid-Interval						
Frequency × Mid-Interval						

A mean passenger

    a) By completing the table, estimate the mean number of passengers.
    b) By plotting a cumulative frequency curve, determine the median value.
    c) What is the modal group?

Q3   40 pupils have taken an exam and their marks are recorded in a frequency table.

Mark (%)	$0 \leqslant m < 20$	$20 \leqslant m < 40$	$40 \leqslant m < 60$	$60 \leqslant m < 80$	$80 \leqslant m < 100$
Frequency	2	12	18	5	3
Cumulative Frequency					
Mid-Interval					

    a) Complete the table and plot the cumulative frequency curve.
    b) What is the value of the lower quartile?
    c) What is the interquartile range?
    d) What is the median mark?

Q4   One hundred scores for a board game are presented in the table below.

Score	31 – 40	41 – 50	51 – 60	61 – 70	71 – 80	81 – 90	91 – 100
Frequency	4	12	21	32	19	8	4
Cumulative Frequency							
Mid-Interval							

    a) What is the modal group?
    b) Which group contains the median score?
    c) By plotting the cumulative frequency curve determine the actual value of the median score.
    d) Find the interquartile range.

Cumulative Frequency

Q5 The following frequency table gives the distribution of the lives of electric bulbs.

a) Complete the frequency table.

Life (hours)	Frequency	Cumulative Frequency	Mid-Interval
900 – 999	10		
1000 – 1099	12		
1100 – 1199	15		
1200 – 1299	18		
1300 – 1399	22		
1400 – 1499	17		
1500 – 1599	14		
1600 – 1699	9		

b) Which group contains the median value?

c) By drawing the cumulative frequency curve, find the actual value of the median.

d) Determine values for the upper and lower quartiles.

Q6 The following box plot shows the ages in years of trees in a wood.

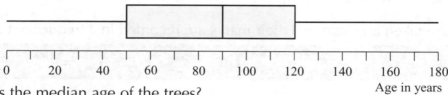

0   20   40   60   80   100   120   140   160   180

Age in years

a) What is the median age of the trees?

b) What is the upper quartile value?

c) What is the interquartile range?

Q7 30 pupils recorded the time taken (minutes : seconds) to boil some water.
Here are their results:
2:37 2:37 3:17 3:30 2:45 2:13 3:18 3:12 3:38 3:29
3:04 3:24 4:13 3:01 3:11 2:33 3:37 4:24 3:59 3:11
3:22 3:13 2:57 3:12 3:07 4:17 3:31 3:42 3:51 3:24

a) By using a tally, transfer the data into the frequency table.

Time	$2:00 \leqslant t < 2:30$	$2:30 \leqslant t < 3:00$	$3:00 \leqslant t < 3:30$	$3:30 \leqslant t < 4:00$	$4:00 \leqslant t < 4:30$
Tally					
Frequency					
Cumulative Frequency					
Mid-Interval					

b) Draw the cumulative frequency curve.

c) Using your graph, read off the median and the upper and lower quartiles.

d) What is the interquartile range?

Histograms

It's the <u>size that counts</u>... You've got to look at the <u>area</u> of the bars, which means looking at the <u>width</u> as well as the height.

Q1 The histogram below represents the age distribution of people that watch outdoor bog snorkelling. Given that there are 24 people in the 40 – 55 age range, find the number of people in all the other age ranges.

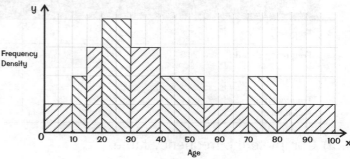

Q2 The weight of honey collected from several beehives is tabulated below.

a) Complete the frequency table by calculating the frequency densities.
b) Draw a histogram to represent this data.
c) Use your histogram to estimate the number of beehives that produced more than 6 kg of honey.

Weight (kg)	0 – 2	3 – 4	5 – 7	8 – 9	10 – 15
Frequency	3	2	6	9	12
Frequency density					

Q3 Match the histograms to their corresponding cumulative frequency curves.

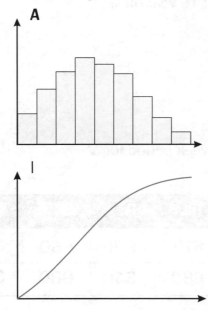

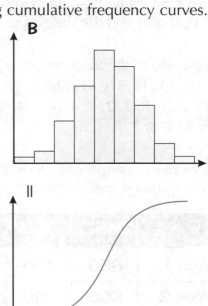

STAGE ONE

Histograms and Dispersion

Know your shapes — they're bound to ask you what different-shaped graphs mean, so get learning.

Q1 The lifetimes of 96 microwaves are tabulated:

Lifetime (years)	$0 \leqslant L < 2$	$2 \leqslant L < 4$	$4 \leqslant L < 6$	$6 \leqslant L < 8$	$8 \leqslant L < 10$	$10 \leqslant L < 12$
Frequency	15	22	36	9	10	4
Frequency density						
Mid-Interval						
Frequency × Mid-Interval						

a) Complete the frequency table.
b) Estimate the mean lifetime.
c) Which group contains the median value?
d) How many lifetimes are outside the modal group?

e) Draw a histogram and use it to determine the number of microwaves with lifetimes shorter than 5 years.

Q2 A group of sixth formers took part in a survey to see how much time they spent watching TV each week.

a) Complete the table by filling in the frequency density column.
b) How many students took part in the survey?
c) Represent the data as a histogram.
d) Estimate the number of students that watch more than 7, but less than 13 hours each week.

No. of hours	Frequency	Frequency density
0 – 1	6	
2 – 3	13	
4 – 5	15	
6 – 8	9	
9 – 10	23	
11 – 15	25	
16 – 20	12	

Q3 Draw two contrasting histograms showing the weights of a sample of eight year olds and the weights of a sample of 16 year olds.

Q4 Find the means of the following data sets:
a) 20, 18, 16, 14, 12, 16, 0, 4, 6, 8
b) 8, 6, 6, 3, 2, 1, 5, 1, 2, 2, 4, 3, 3, 4, 3
c) 10, 9, 8, 8, 8, 8, 7, 7, 4, 3.

Q5 The daily sales of petrol, in gallons, during a 2-week period for a petrol filling station are as follows:

	Mon	Tue	Wed	Thur	Fri	Sat	Sun
Week 1	650	310	540	570	630	660	300
Week 2	550	310	490	560	540	680	340

Which is greater, the mean value for week 1 or for week 2?

Histograms and Dispersion

Q6   A farmer keeps track of the amount of milk produced by his cows each day.

Amount of Milk (Litres)	Frequency	Frequency Density	Mid-Interval	Frequency × Mid-Interval
$0 < C < 1$	6			
$1 \leqslant C < 5$	6			
$5 < C < 8$	6			
$8 \leqslant C < 10$	6			
$10 < C < 15$	6			
$15 < C < 20$	6			

a) Complete the frequency table.

b) Use the mid-interval technique to estimate the mean.

c) Draw a histogram to show the data.

d) On how many days is less than 8 litres produced?

Q7   Find the means of the following data sets.

a) -2, -4, 4, 6, -10, 10

b) 21, 23, 19, 22, 21, 23, 20, 22

c) 579, 791, 3989, 184, 369

d) 87, 42, 53, 35, 61, 36

e) -56, -23, -93, -70, -22, -30

f) $2^1, 2^2, 2^3, 2^4, 2^5$

Q8   A magazine has carried out a survey to see how much pocket money its readers receive each week.

Amount (£)	Frequency	Frequency Density	Mid-Interval	Frequency × Mid-Interval
0 — 0.50	11			
0.60 — 0.90	25			
1.00 — 1.20	9			
1.30 — 1.40	12			
1.50 — 1.70	24			
1.80 — 2.40	21			
2.50 — 3.00	54			
3.10 — 4.00	32			

a) By first completing the table, estimate the mean amount of pocket money.

b) What is the modal class?

c) Draw a histogram to represent the data.

d) How many readers receive more than £1.35 each week?

Scatter Graphs

A __SCATTER GRAPH__ is just a load of points on a graph that <u>end up in a bit of a</u> <u>mess</u>, rather than in a nice line or curve. There's a fancy word to say how much of a mess they're in — it's __CORRELATION__.

__Q1__ Match the following diagrams with the most appropriate descriptive label.

Labels:
(P) Strong positive correlation   (S) Moderate negative correlation
(Q) Exact negative correlation   (T) Medium correlation
(R) Little or no correlation   (U) Exact positive correlation.

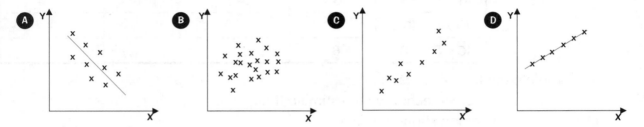

__Q2__ 8 friends are comparing heights and shoe sizes to see if they are correlated. The data is tabulated below:

Height	4'6"	4'8"	5'2"	5'5"	5'8"	5'10"	6'	6'6"
Shoe size	4	5	4.5	5	6	8	9	12

__a)__ Plot the points on a scatter graph.

__b)__ Are the points positively or negatively correlated?

__c)__ By fitting an appropriate line, estimate the shoe size of another friend who is 6'2".

__Q3__ Janine is convinced that the more expensive cookery books contain more pages. To test out her theory, she has compiled this table:

Price	£4.25	£5.00	£4.75	£6.25	£7.50	£8.25	£4.75	£5.00	£6.75	£3.25	£3.75
No. of pages	172	202	118	184	278	328	158	138	268	84	98

__a)__ Draw a scatter graph to represent this information.

__b)__ Draw in a line of best fit.

__c)__ Use your line to estimate the price of a book containing 250 pages.

__Q4__ A local electrical store has kept a log of the number of CD players sold at each price:

Price (£)	£80	£150	£230	£310	£380	£460
No. Sold	27	24	22	19	17	15

__a)__ Draw this information as a scatter graph, using suitable axes.

__b)__ Draw a line of best fit and use it to estimate:

    __i)__ the number of CD players the shopkeeper could expect to sell for £280

    __ii)__ how much the shopkeeper should charge if he wanted to sell exactly 20 CD players.

__c)__ Is the data positively or negatively correlated?

Sampling Methods

Q1 Define:
  a) random sampling
  b) systematic sampling
  c) stratified sampling

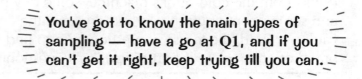

You've got to know the main types of sampling — have a go at Q1, and if you can't get it right, keep trying till you can.

You've also got to be able to spot problems and criticise sampling techniques — basically, if you think it's a load of rubbish, you get the chance to say why.

Q2 Give a reason why the following methods of sampling are poor:
  a) a survey carried out inside a newsagents concluded that 80% of the population buy a daily newspaper
  b) a phone poll conducted at 11 am on a Sunday morning revealed that less than 2% of the population regularly go to church
  c) 60% of the population were estimated to watch the 9 o'clock news each evening after a survey was carried out at a bridge club.

Q3 Decide which of the following questions (if any) are suitable for a survey to find which of five desserts (cheesecake, fruit salad, sherry trifle, knickerbocker glory and chocolate cake) people like the most. Give a reason for each of your answers.
  a) Do you like cheesecake, fruit salad, sherry trifle, knickerbocker glory or chocolate cake?
  b) How often do you eat dessert?
  c) Which is your favourite out of: cheesecake; fruit salad; sherry trifle; knickerbocker glory; chocolate cake.
  d) What is your favourite dessert?
  e) Is your favourite dessert: cheesecake; fruit salad; sherry trifle; knickerbocker glory; chocolate cake; none of these.

Q4 A newspaper contained the following article regarding the amount of exercise teenagers take outside school.

  a) Suggest 3 questions that you could use in a survey to find out whether this is true at your school.
  b) At a particular school there are 300 pupils in each of years 7 to 11. There are approximately equal numbers of girls and boys.
  Describe how you would select 10% of the pupils for a stratified sample which is representative of all the pupils at the school.

Over half of all teenagers do no exercise at all. Only one in ten play team sports or take part in individual sports.
blah-blah-blah-blah-blah blah-blah-blah-blah-blah blah-blah-blah-blah-blah blah-blah-blah-blah-blah blah-blah-blah-blah-blah blah-blah-blah-blah-blah blah-blah-blah-blah-blah blah-blah-blah-blah-blah blah-blah-blah-blah-blah blah-blah-blah-blah-blah

Sampling Methods

Q5 Pauline is the manager of a small café. She knows that some of her customers buy cold drinks from the cold drinks machine, some buy hot drinks from the hot drinks machine and some people buy snacks and drinks at the counter.

Pauline would like to use a questionnaire to find out whether she should stock a new brand of cola. Here is part of Pauline's questionnaire:

Cafe Questionnaire

1) Please tick the box to show how often you visit the café:

daily ☐   weekly ☐   fortnightly ☐   monthly ☐   less than monthly ☐

a) Using the same style, design another question that Pauline can include in her questionnaire.

b) Pauline hands out her questionnaire as she serves customers at the counter. Give a reason why this is a suitable or unsuitable way to hand out the questionnaire.

Statistics Crossword

ACROSS

1) You can easily find the range and average from this type of table. (9)

5) A method of sampling which tries to use the same proportions as the whole population. (5)

7) There's more than one layer to this sort of sampling. (10)

8) It's not a matter of being cruel, its just a way of working out averages. (4)

9) With so many choices no wonder these diagrams branch off in so many directions. (4)

DOWN

2) Adding it up as you go along. (10)

3) Distance from the lowest to highest. (5)

4) This graph is more scat. (7)

6) It's not the height but the area of each bar that matters with this type of chart. (9)

8) Perhaps the most common way of finding an average. (4)

Time Series

Time Series — don't you just love 'em. These little horrors are pretty important, and could easily raise their ugly head in the Exam. Do yourself a favour and practise them.

Q1 Which of the following sets of measurements form time series?
a) The average rainfall in Cumbria, measured each day for a year.
b) The daily rainfall in European capital cities on Christmas Day, 2000.
c) The shoe size of everybody in Class 6C on September 1st, 2001.
d) My shoe size (measured every month) from when I was twelve months old to when I was fourteen years old.

Q2 **a)** Which two of the following time series are seasonal, and which two are not seasonal?

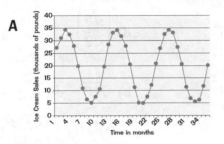

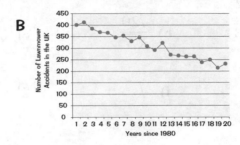

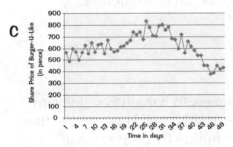

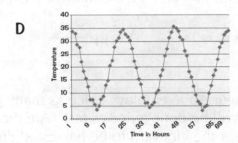

b) What are the periods of the time series which are seasonal?
c) Describe the trends in the time series which are **not** seasonal.

Q3 The following table shows the value of a knitwear company's sock sales in the years 1998-2000. The sales figures are given in thousands of pounds.

Time	Sales		
Spring 1998	404		
Summer 1998	401		
Autumn 1998	411		
Winter 1998	420		
Spring 1999	416		
Summer 1999	409		
Autumn 1999	419		
Winter 1999	424		
Spring 2000	416		
Summer 2000	413		
Autumn 2000	427		
Winter 2000	440		

a) Plot the figures on a graph with time on the horizontal axis and sales on the vertical axis.
b) Calculate a 4-point moving average to smooth the series. Copy the table and write your answers in the empty boxes.
c) Plot the moving average on the same axes as your original graph.
d) Describe the trend of the sales figures.

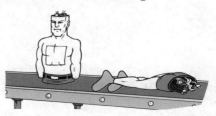

STAGE TWO

Surds Mostly

Q1   Write down the reciprocals of the following values.
Leave your answers as whole numbers or fractions.

a) 7   **b)** 12   **c)** $\dfrac{3}{8}$ **d)** $-\dfrac{1}{2}$

Q2   Use your calculator to work out the reciprocals of the following values.
Write your answers as whole numbers or decimals.

a) 12   **b)** $\sqrt{2}$ **c)** π **d)** 0.008

Q3   Simplify:

a) $\sqrt{5} \times \sqrt{3}$ **b)** $\dfrac{\sqrt{20}}{\sqrt{5}}$ **c)** $\sqrt{4} - \sqrt{1}$ **d)** $\left(\dfrac{\sqrt{5}}{\sqrt{2}}\right)^2$

e) $\left(\sqrt{x}\right)^2$ **f)** $\sqrt{x^2}$ **g)** $\sqrt{8} \times \sqrt{8}$ **h)** $\sqrt{18} - \sqrt{9}$

Q4   If $x = 1$ and $y = \sqrt{2}$, are the following expressions rational or irrational?

a) $(x+y)(x-y)$ **b)** $\dfrac{x+y}{x-y}$

Q5   If Monsieur Abbé employs twice as many grape-pickers to harvest his vineyard,
the job will be done twice as fast. Are the number of grape-pickers and the time
it takes for the vineyard to be harvested **directly** or **indirectly** proportional?

Q6   Rationalise the denominators of the following expressions, and then
simplify if necessary.

a) $\dfrac{1}{\sqrt{2}}$ **b)** $\dfrac{2}{\sqrt{8}}$ **c)** $\dfrac{a}{\frac{\sqrt{40}}{2}}$ **d)** $\dfrac{x}{\sqrt{xy}}$

e) $\dfrac{1}{1+\sqrt{2}}$ **f)** $\dfrac{6}{3+\sqrt{3}}$ **g)** $\dfrac{2}{1+\sqrt{6}}$ **h)** $\dfrac{5+\sqrt{5}}{5-\sqrt{5}}$

**Remember: rationalising the denominator means getting
rid of the square root signs on the bottom of fractions.**

Q7   Over a five-month period, Louise spends £450 on petrol.
How much does she spend a year on petrol?

**Try working out how much she spends in *one* month on
petrol, and then times that by 12 to get the annual total.**

Q8   A circle has a radius of $\sqrt{3}$ cm. What is its exact area? (Area of circle $= \pi r^2$)

Rounding Off

Rounding a number off to a certain number of decimal places or significant figures is really quite easy — the tricky bit's when they ask for minimum and maximum values...

Q1 Calculate, giving your answers to a sensible degree of accuracy:

a) $\dfrac{42.65 \times 0.9863}{24.6 \times 2.43}$

b) $\dfrac{13.63 + 7.22}{13.63 - 7.22}$

Remember — the real value could be anything up to half a unit above or below the rounded off value.

Q2 $R = \dfrac{S}{T}$ is a formula used by stockbrokers.

$S = 940$, correct to 2 significant figures and $T = 5.56$, correct to 3 significant figures.

a) For the value of S, write down the upper bound and the lower bound.

b) For the value of T, write down the upper bound and the lower bound.

c) Calculate the upper bound and lower bound for R.

d) Write down the value of R correct to an appropriate number of significant figures.

The trick to find the maximum/minimum of a calculation is to work out the max/min values of each bit, then use both in the calculation.

Q3 **a)** The length of a rectangle is measured as 12 ± 0.1 cm. The width of the same rectangle is measured as 4 ± 0.1 cm. Calculate the perimeter of the rectangle, giving also the maximum possible error.

b) A rectangle measures $A \pm x$ cm in length and $B \pm y$ cm in width. The formula $P = 2(A + B)$ is used to calculate the perimeter, P, of the rectangle. What is the maximum possible error in P?

Q4 Thomas is using his new calculator. He presses $\sqrt{}$ then 8.

What is the answer correct to two decimal places?

Q5 Calculate, giving your answers to a sensible degree of accuracy:

a) $\dfrac{18.95 \times 0.6464}{2.4 - 2.0}$ **b)** $\dfrac{324 + 7.22}{243 - 7.2}$

Q6 Jodie weighs herself on some scales that are accurate to the nearest 10 grams. The digital display shows her weight as 64.78 kg.

a) What is the maximum that she could weigh?

b) What is the minimum that she could weigh?

Upper/Lower Bounds are just another way of saying the Maximum/Minimum possible values.

Q7 $A = 13$, correct to 2 significant figures.
$B = 12.5$, correct to 3 significant figures.

a) For the value of A, write down the upper bound and the lower bound.

b) For the value of B, write down the upper bound and the lower bound.

c) Calculate the upper bound and lower bound for C when $C = AB$.

Algebraic Fractions & D.O.T.S.

Q1   Using the fact that $a^2 - b^2 = (a + b)(a - b)$, factorise the following expressions:

a) $x^2 - 9$

b) $y^2 - 16$

c) $25 - z^2$

d) $36 - a^2$

e) $4x^2 - 9$

f) $9y^2 - 4$

g) $25 - 16z^2$

h) $1 - 36a^2$

i) $x^4 - 36$

j) $x^4 - y^4$

k) $1 - (ab)^2$

l) $100\,x^2 - 144y^2$

$(x + 3)(x - 3)$

Q2   Simplify the following by cancelling down where possible:

a) $\dfrac{27x^4y^2z}{9x^3yz^2}$

b) $\dfrac{48a^2b^2}{(2a)^2c}$

c) $\dfrac{3xyz}{9x^2y^3z^4}$

d) $\dfrac{4p^3q^3}{(2pr)^3}$

Q3   Multiply out the following, leaving your answers as simplified as possible:

a) $\dfrac{x^2}{y} \times \dfrac{2}{x^3}$

b) $\dfrac{3a^4}{2} \times \dfrac{b}{a^2}$

c) $\dfrac{2x}{y^2} \times \dfrac{y^3}{4x^3}$

d) $\dfrac{3pq}{2} \times \dfrac{4r^2}{9p}$

e) $\dfrac{10z^3}{xy} \times \dfrac{4x^3}{5z}$

f) $\dfrac{30a^2b^2c^2}{7} \times \dfrac{21c^2}{ab^3}$

g) $\dfrac{4}{x} \times \dfrac{x^3}{2} \times \dfrac{x}{10}$

h) $\dfrac{2a^2}{3} \times \dfrac{9b}{a} \times \dfrac{2a^2b}{5}$

i) $\dfrac{5a^2b}{b} \times \dfrac{3a^2c^3}{10bd}$

j) $\dfrac{p^2}{pq^2} \times \dfrac{q^2}{p}$

k) $\dfrac{90r^2}{14t} \times \dfrac{7t^3}{30r}$

l) $\dfrac{400d^4}{51e^5} \times \dfrac{102d^2e^4}{800e^2f}$

Q4   Divide the following, leaving your answer as simplified as possible:

a) $\dfrac{4x^3}{y} \div \dfrac{2x}{y^2}$

b) $\dfrac{ab}{c} \div \dfrac{b}{c}$

c) $\dfrac{30x^3}{y^2} \div \dfrac{10x}{y}$

d) $\dfrac{pq}{r} \div \dfrac{2}{r}$

e) $\dfrac{e^2f^2}{5} \div \dfrac{ef}{10}$

f) $\dfrac{5x^3}{y} \div \dfrac{1}{y}$

g) $\dfrac{16xyz}{3} \div \dfrac{4x^2}{9}$

h) $\dfrac{20a^3}{b^3} \div \dfrac{5}{b^2}$

i) $\dfrac{25a^3}{b^3} \div \dfrac{5}{b^2}$

j) $\dfrac{4x}{y^4z^4} \div \dfrac{2}{y^2z^3}$

k) $\dfrac{3m}{2n^2} \div \dfrac{m}{4n}$

l) $\dfrac{70f^3}{g} \div \dfrac{10f^4}{g^2}$

Q5   Solve the following equations for x:

a) $\dfrac{20x^4y^2z^3}{7xy^5} \times \dfrac{14y^3}{40x^2z^3} = 5$

b) $\dfrac{48x^5y^2}{12z^3} \div \dfrac{16x^2y^2}{z^3} = 2$

Q6   Factorise:

a) $x^2 - 4$

b) $144 - y^4$

c) $1 - 9x^2y^2$

d) $49x^4y^4 - 1$

STAGE TWO

Algebraic Fractions

OK, I guess it gets a bit tricky here — you've got to cross-multiply to get a common denominator before you can get anywhere with adding or subtracting.

Q1 Add the following, simplifying your answers:

a) $\dfrac{3}{2x} + \dfrac{y}{2x}$

e) $\dfrac{5x+2}{x} + \dfrac{2x+4}{x}$

i) $\dfrac{2x}{3} + \dfrac{2x}{4}$

b) $\dfrac{1}{x} + \dfrac{y}{x}$

f) $\dfrac{6x}{3} + \dfrac{2x+y}{6}$

j) $\dfrac{x}{6} + \dfrac{5x}{7}$

c) $\dfrac{4xy}{3z} + \dfrac{2xy}{3z}$

g) $\dfrac{x}{8} + \dfrac{2+y}{24}$

k) $\dfrac{x}{3} + \dfrac{x}{y}$

d) $\dfrac{(4x+2)}{3} + \dfrac{(2x-1)}{3}$

h) $\dfrac{x}{10} + \dfrac{y-1}{5}$

l) $\dfrac{zx}{4} + \dfrac{x+z}{y}$

Q2 Subtract the following, leaving your answers as simplified as possible:

a) $\dfrac{4x}{3} - \dfrac{5y}{3}$

e) $\dfrac{10+x^2}{4x} - \dfrac{x^2+11}{4x}$

i) $\dfrac{2b}{a} - \dfrac{b}{7}$

b) $\dfrac{4x+3}{y} - \dfrac{4}{y}$

f) $\dfrac{2x}{3} - \dfrac{y}{6}$

j) $\dfrac{(p+q)}{2} - \dfrac{3p}{5}$

c) $\dfrac{(8x+3y)}{2x} - \dfrac{(4x+2)}{2x}$

g) $\dfrac{z}{5} - \dfrac{2z}{15}$

k) $\dfrac{p-2q}{4} - \dfrac{2p+q}{2}$

d) $\dfrac{(9-5x)}{3x} - \dfrac{(3+x)}{3x}$

h) $\dfrac{4m}{n} - \dfrac{m}{3}$

l) $\dfrac{3x}{y} - \dfrac{4-x}{3}$

Q3 Simplify the following:

a) $\left(\dfrac{a}{b} \div \dfrac{c}{d}\right) \times \dfrac{ac}{bd}$

d) $\dfrac{m^2n}{p} + \dfrac{mn}{p^2}$

g) $\dfrac{a+b}{a-b} + \dfrac{a-b}{a+b}$

b) $\dfrac{x^2+xy}{x} \times \dfrac{z}{xz+yz}$

e) $\dfrac{1}{x+y} + \dfrac{1}{x-y}$

h) $\dfrac{1}{4pq} \div \dfrac{1}{3pq}$

c) $\dfrac{(p+q)}{r} \times \dfrac{3}{2(p+q)}$

f) $\dfrac{2}{x} - \dfrac{3}{2x} + \dfrac{4}{3x}$

i) $\dfrac{x}{8} - \dfrac{x+y}{4} + \dfrac{x-y}{2}$

Rearranging Formulas

Rearranging is getting the letter you want out of the formula and making it the subject. And it's exactly the same method as for solving equations, which can't be bad.

Q1 Rearrange the following formulas to make the letter in brackets the new subject.

a) $g = 10 - 4h$ (h)

b) $d = \frac{1}{2}(c + 4)$ (c)

c) $j = -2(3 - k)$ (k)

d) $a = \dfrac{2b}{3}$ (b)

e) $f = \dfrac{3g}{8}$ (g)

f) $y = \dfrac{x}{2} - 3$ (x)

g) $s = \dfrac{t}{6} + 10$ (t)

h) $p = 4q^2$ (q)

Q2 A car salesperson is paid £w for working m months and selling c cars, where
$$w = 500m + 50c$$
a) Rearrange the formula to make c the subject.
b) Find the number of cars the salesperson sells in 11 months if he earns £12,100 during that time.

Q3 The cost of hiring a car is £28 per day plus 25p per mile.
a) Find the cost of hiring the car and travelling:

   i) 40 miles.
   ii) 80 miles.

b) Write down a formula to give the cost of hiring a car (£) for one day, and travelling n miles.
c) Rearrange the formula to make n the subject.
d) How many miles can you travel, during one day, if you have a budget of:

   i) £34, **ii)** £50, **iii)** £56.50?

Q4 Rearrange the following formulas to make the letter in brackets the new subject.

a) $y = x^2 - 2$ (x)

b) $y = \sqrt{(x + 3)}$ (x)

c) $r = \left(\dfrac{s}{2}\right)^2$ (s)

d) $f = \dfrac{10 + g}{3}$ (g)

e) $w = \dfrac{5 - z}{2}$ (z)

f) $V = \frac{1}{3} x^2 h$ (x)

g) $v^2 = u^2 + 2as$ (a)

h) $v^2 = u^2 + 2as$ (u)

i) $t^2 = 2\pi\sqrt{\dfrac{1}{g}}$ (g)

Q5 Mrs Smith buys x jumpers for £J each and sells them in her shop for a total price of £T.
a) Write down an expression for the amount of money she paid for all the jumpers.
b) Using your answer to **a)**, write down a formula for the profit £P Mrs Smith makes selling all the jumpers.
c) Rearrange the formula to make J the subject.
d) Given that Mrs Smith makes a profit of £156 by selling 13 jumpers for a total of £364, find the price she paid for each jumper originally.

Rearranging Formulas

Q6 The cost of developing a film is 12p per print plus 60p postage.

    a) Find the cost of developing a film with:

      i) 12 prints.
      ii) 24 prints.

    b) Write down a formula for the cost C, in pence, of developing x prints.
    c) Rearrange the formula to make x the subject.
    d) Find the number of prints developed when a customer is charged:

      i) £4.92
      ii) £6.36
      iii) £12.12.

Q7 Rearrange the following formulas, by collecting terms in x and looking for common factors, to make x the new subject.

    a) $xy = z - 2x$
    b) $ax = 3x + b$
    c) $4x - y = xz$
    d) $xy = 3z - 5x + y$

    e) $xy = xz - 2$
    f) $2(x - y) = z(x + 3)$
    g) $xyz = x - y - wz$
    h) $3y(x + z) = y(2z - x)$

These are getting quite tricky — you've got to <u>collect like terms</u>, before you can make anything else the subject.

Q8 Rearrange the following to make the letter in brackets the new subject.

    a) $pq = 3p + 4r - 2q$ (p)

    b) $fg + 2e = 5 - 2g$ (g)

    c) $a(b - 2) = c(b + 3)$ (b)

    d) $pq^2 = rq^2 + 4$ (q)

    e) $4(a - b) + c(a - 2) = ad$ (a)

    f) $\dfrac{x^2}{3} - y = x^2$ (x)

    g) $hk^2 = 14 + k^2$ (k)

    h) $2\sqrt{x} + y = z\sqrt{x} + 4$ (x)

    i) $\dfrac{a}{b} = \dfrac{1}{3}(b - a)$ (a)

    j) $\dfrac{m + n}{m - n} = \dfrac{3}{4}$ (m)

    k) $\sqrt{\dfrac{(d - e)}{e}} = 7$ (e)

    l) $\dfrac{x - 2y}{xy} = 3$ (y)

Q9 Rearrange the following formulas to make y the new subject.

    a) $x(y - 1) = y$

    b) $x(y + 2) = y - 3$

    c) $x = \dfrac{y^2 + 1}{2y^2 - 1}$

    d) $x = \dfrac{2y^2 + 1}{3y^2 - 2}$

Simultaneous Equations

To solve simultaneous equations from scratch, you've got to get rid of either *x* or *y* first — to leave you with an equation with just one unknown in it.

Q1 Eliminate either the *x* term or the *y* term by adding or subtracting the pairs of equations, and hence solve the equations:

a) $4x - y = 13$
$2x - y = 5$

b) $8x + 3y = 8$
$5x - 3y = 5$

c) $x + 3y = 10$
$2x - 3y = 2$

d) $8x + 6y = 2$
$2(x - 3y) = 3$

e) $x - 12y = 16$
$5x + 12y = 8$

f) $2(5x - y + 4) = 0$
$10x + y = 19$

g) $11x + 3y = 5$
$7x - 3y = 13$

h) $2x + 7y = 11$
$2x + 3y = 7$

i) $x + 6y = 5$
$3(x + 2y - 1) = 0$

Q2 Rearrange the equations before solving for *x* and *y*:

a) $3y - 4x = 10$
$4(x - \frac{y}{2} + 2) = 0$

b) $3x + y = 13$
$2y - 3x = 8$

c) $3y + 4x = 10$
$4x - 2y + 8 = 0$

d) $y + 1 = 3x$
$y - x = 3$

e) $y + x = 2$
$y - \frac{1}{2}x + 1 = 0$

f) $y - 3 = 2x$
$y = x - 1$

g) $4y - 3x = 22$
$3x - 2y = -14$

h) $y + 2x = 5$
$y = x - 4$

i) $2y + x = 2$
$y + x + 1 = 0$

j) $3y + 2x = 19$
$2x + y = 1$

k) $9x - y = 12$
$4y - 9x = 6$

l) $6x + 2y = 5$
$3y - 6x = 15$

Q3 Multiply one equation by a number before adding or subtracting. Solve the equations:

a) $3x + 2y = 12$
$2x + y = 7$

b) $5x - y = 17$
$2x + 3y = 0$

c) $x + 3y = 11$
$2x + 5y = 19$

d) $5x + 3y = 24$
$x + 5y = -4$

e) $3x + 2y = 3$
$2x + y = 23$

f) $4x + 2y = 8$
$x + 3y = 2$

g) $x + 14y = -2$
$2x + 3y = 21$

h) $3x + 2y = 21$
$2x - y = 7$

i) $4x - y = -2$
$3x - 2y = 1$

Q4 Multiply both equations by a number before adding or subtracting, to solve these:

a) $7y - 3x = 2$
$5y - 2x = 2$

b) $5x - 8y = 12$
$4x - 7y = 9$

c) $4x - 2y = -6$
$5x + 3y = 20$

d) $7x + 5y = 66$
$3x - 4y = 16$

e) $10x + 4y = 2$
$8x + 3y = 1$

f) $3x + 4y = 19$
$4x - 3y = -8$

Q5 Use the linear equation (the one with no *x²*s in it) to find an expression for *y*. Then substitute it into the quadratic equation (the one <u>with</u> *x²*s in it), to solve these equations:

a) $y = x^2 + 2$
$y = x + 14$

b) $y = x^2 - 8$
$y = 3x + 10$

c) $y = 2x^2$
$y = x + 3$

d) $x + 5y = 30$
$x^2 + \frac{4}{5}x = y$

e) $y = 1 - 13x$
$y = 4x^2 + 4$

f) $y = 3(x^2 + 3)$
$14x + y = 1$

For question 5, you'll get two possible values for *x*.
Which means you'll also have two possible values for *y*...

Simultaneous Equations and Graphs

 This is a nice easy way of solving simultaneous equations. All you've got to do is draw
2 straight-line graphs and read off a value where they cross each other.
It does mean you've got to be up to speed with your straight-line graphs, though...

Q1 The simultaneous equations given below have been plotted as straight-line graphs.
Write down the solutions of the simultaneous equations by looking at the graphs.
Finally check your answers by substituting them back into the simultaneous equations.

a) $y + 2x = 9$
$3y = x + 6$

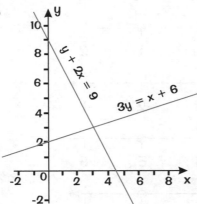

b) $y + x = 1$
$3y = x + 11$

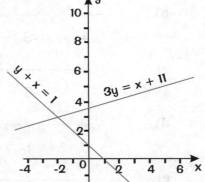

c) $y = 2x - 13$
$2y + x + 6 = 0$

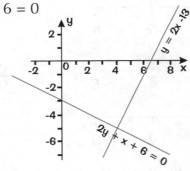

d) $2y = 8 - x$
$2y = x - 2$

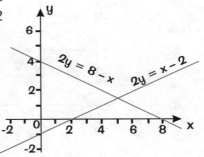

Q2 For each pair of simultaneous equations below:
i) draw and label a pair of axes with x from -3 to 7, and y from -6 to 6
ii) complete two tables of values
iii) plot two straight-line graphs onto your axes, remembering to label each graph
iv) use your graphs to find the values of x and y that fit both equations.
v) check your answers by substituting them into both of the equations.

a) $y = x + 2$
$y = 3x - 2$

b) $y = 2x - 2$
$2y = x + 8$

c) $y = x + 1$
$y = 2x - 2$

d) $y = x + 3$
$y = 3x - 1$

e) $y = 2x + 3$
$y = x - 1$

f) $y = 2 - x$
$y = \frac{1}{2}x - 1$

g) $y = x - 1$
$2y = x + 1$

h) $y + 2 = 4x$
$y + x = 3$

i) $y + 2 = x$
$y = \frac{1}{2}x + 1$

STAGE TWO

Inequalities

Yet another one of those bits of Maths that looks worse than it is —
these are just like equations, really, except for the symbols.

Q1 Write down the inequality represented by each diagram below.

a)
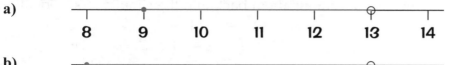

| | | | | | | |
|8|9|10|11|12|13|14|

b)
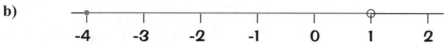

| | | | | | | |
|-4|-3|-2|-1|0|1|2|

c)
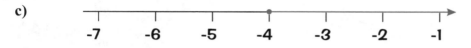

| | | | | | | |
|-7|-6|-5|-4|-3|-2|-1|

d)
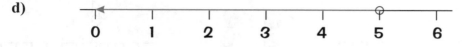

| | | | | | | |
|0|1|2|3|4|5|6|

e)
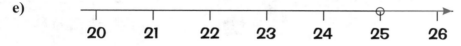

| | | | | | | |
|20|21|22|23|24|25|26|

f)
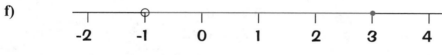

| | | | | | | |
|-2|-1|0|1|2|3|4|

g)
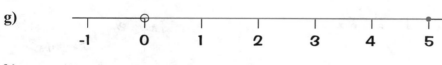

| | | | | | | |
|-1|0|1|2|3|4|5|

h)
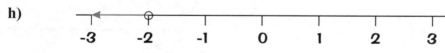

| | | | | | | |
|-3|-2|-1|0|1|2|3|

Q2 By drawing an appropriate part of the number line for each question, represent each of the following inequalities.

a) $x > 5$

b) $x \leq 2$

c) $2 > x > -5$

d) $3 > x \geq -2$

e) $3 \geq x > -2$

f) $7 \geq x > 6$

g) $-3 \leq x \leq -2$

h) $0 \geq x > -3$

Q3 Draw and label a number line from –5 to 5 for each of the following questions. Represent the inequalities on your number lines.

a) $x^2 \leq 4$

b) $x^2 < 1$

c) $x^2 \leq 9$

d) $25 \geq x^2$

e) $16 \geq x^2$

f) $x^2 \leq 1$

g) $9 > x^2$

h) $x^2 \leq 0$

Q4 Solve the following:

a) $3x + 2 > 11$

b) $5x + 4 < 24$

c) $5x + 7 \leq 32$

d) $3x + 12 \leq 30$

e) $2x - 7 \geq 8$

f) $17 + 4x < 33$

g) $2(x + 3) < 20$

h) $2(5x - 4) < 32$

i) $5(x + 2) \geq 25$

j) $4(x - 1) > 40$

k) $10 - 2x > 4x - 8$

l) $7 - 2x \leq 4x + 10$

m) $8 - 3x \geq 14$

n) $16 - x < 11$

o) $16 - x > 1$

p) $12 - 3x \leq 18$

Inequalities

Q5 There are 1,130 pupils in a school. No class must have more than 32 pupils. How many classrooms should be used? Show this information as an inequality.

Q6 A person is prepared to spend £300 taking friends out for a meal. If the restaurant charges £12 per head, how many guests could be invited? Show this information as an inequality.

Q7 Find the largest integer x, such that $2x + 5 \geq 5x - 2$.

Q8 When a number is subtracted from 11, and this new number is then divided by two, the result is always less than five. Write this information as an inequality and solve it to show the possible values of the number.

Q9 The shaded region satisfies three inequalities. Write down these inequalities.

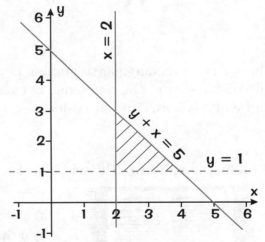

Q10 Draw a set of axes with the x-axis from –2 to 6 and the y-axis from –1 to 7. Show on a graph the region enclosed by the following three inequalities.

$$y < 6 \quad , \quad x + y \geq 5 \quad \text{and} \quad x \leq 5$$

Q11 Draw a set of axes with the x-axis from 0 to 8 and the y-axis from 0 to 10. Show on a graph the region enclosed by the following three inequalities.

$$x > 1 \quad , \quad x + y \leq 7 \quad \text{and} \quad y \geq 2$$

Q12 Draw a set of axes with the x-axis from –4 to 5 and the y-axis from –3 to 6. Show on a graph the region enclosed by the following.

$$y \leq 2x + 4 \quad , \quad y < 5 - x \quad \text{and} \quad y \geq \frac{x}{3} - 1$$

If you're not 100% sure about all this stuff on inequalities, have a look at P.59 of the Revision Guide.

STAGE TWO

Factorising Quadratics

Q1   Factorise the quadratics first, and then solve the equations:

a) $x^2 + 3x - 10 = 0$ d) $x^2 - 4x + 3 = 0$ g) $x^2 + 6x - 7 = 0$

b) $x^2 - 5x + 6 = 0$ e) $x^2 - x - 20 = 0$ h) $x^2 + 14x + 49 = 0$

c) $x^2 - 2x + 1 = 0$ f) $x^2 - 4x - 5 = 0$ i) $x^2 - 2x - 15 = 0$.

Q2   Rearrange into the form "$x^2 + bx + c = 0$", then solve by factorising:

a) $x^2 + 6x = 16$ f) $x^2 - 21 = 4x$ k) $x + 4 - \dfrac{21}{x} = 0$

b) $x^2 + 5x = 36$ g) $x^2 - 300 = 20x$ l) $x(x - 3) = 10$

c) $x^2 + 4x = 45$ h) $x^2 + 48 = 26x$ m) $x^2 - 3(x + 6) = 0$

d) $x^2 = 5x$ i) $x^2 + 36 = 13x$ n) $x - \dfrac{63}{x} = 2$

e) $x^2 = 11x$ j) $x + 5 - \dfrac{14}{x} = 0$ o) $x + 1 = \dfrac{12}{x}$.

Q3   The area of a rectangular swimming pool is 28 m². The width is x m. The difference between the length and width is 3 m. Find the value of x.

Q4   A rug has length x m. The width is exactly 1 m less than the length.

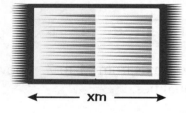

a) Write down an expression for the area of the rug.

b) If the area of the rug is 6 m², find the value of x.

Q5   Solve $x^2 - \frac{1}{4} = 0$.

Q6   A triangle has height $(x + 1)$ cm and a base of $2x$ cm.

a) Write down an expression for the area of the triangle and simplify it.

b) If the area of the triangle is 12 cm², find the value of x.

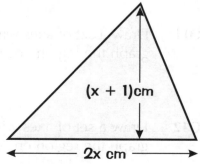

Q7   A square room has a floor of sides x metres. The height of the walls is 3 m. Write down an expression for:

a) the floor area

b) the area of all four walls.

c) If the total area of the floor and the four walls is 64 m², form a quadratic equation and solve it to find x.

The Quadratic Formula

Q1 The following quadratics can be solved by factorisation, but practise using the formula to solve them.

a) $x^2 + 8x + 12 = 0$

b) $6x^2 - x - 2 = 0$

c) $x^2 - x - 6 = 0$

d) $x^2 - 3x + 2 = 0$

e) $4x^2 - 15x + 9 = 0$

f) $x^2 - 3x = 0$

g) $36x^2 - 48x + 16 = 0$

h) $3x^2 + 8x = 0$

i) $2x^2 - 7x - 4 = 0$

j) $x^2 + x - 20 = 0$

k) $4x^2 + 8x - 12 = 0$

l) $3x^2 - 11x - 20 = 0$

m) $x + 3 = 2x^2$

n) $5 - 3x - 2x^2 = 0$

o) $1 - 5x + 6x^2 = 0$

p) $3(x^2 + 2x) = 9$

q) $x^2 + 4(x - 3) = 0$

r) $x^2 = 2(4 - x)$

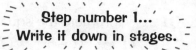

Step number 1...
Write it down in stages.

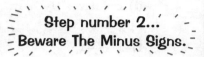

Step number 2...
Beware The Minus Signs.

Step number 3... divide <u>the whole</u> of the top line by **2a**, <u>not just ½ of it</u> — and remember it's **2a**, not just **a**.

Q2 Rearrange the following in the form "$ax^2 + bx + c = 0$" and then solve by the quadratic formula. Give your answers to two decimal places.

a) $x^2 = 8 - 3x$

b) $(x + 2)^2 - 3 = 0$

c) $3x(x - 1) = 5$

d) $2x(x + 4) = 1$

e) $x^2 = 4(x + 1)$

f) $(2x - 1)^2 = 5$

g) $3x^2 + 2x = 6$

h) $(x + 2)(x + 3) = 5$

i) $(x - 2)(2x - 1) = 3$

j) $2x + \frac{4}{x} = 7$

k) $(x - \frac{1}{2})^2 = \frac{1}{4}$

l) $4x(x - 2) = -3$

Pythagoras... remember him — you know, that bloke who didn't like angles.

Q3 The sides of a right-angled triangle are as shown. Use Pythagoras' theorem to form a quadratic equation in x and then solve it to find x.

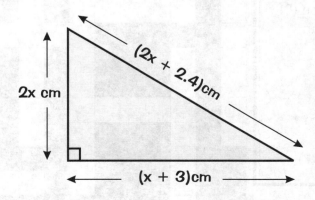

2x cm, (2x + 2.4)cm, (x + 3)cm

Completing the Square

All you're doing is writing it in the form "$(x + 4)^2 + 2$" instead of "$x^2 + 8x + 18$" — don't let the name put you off.

Q1 Complete the square for the following expressions:

a) $x^2 - 4x - 5$

b) $x^2 - 2x + 1$

c) $x^2 + x + 1$

d) $x^2 - 6x + 9$

e) $x^2 - 6x + 7$

f) $x^2 - 4x$

g) $x^2 + 3x - 4$

h) $x^2 - x - 3$

i) $x^2 - 10x + 25$

j) $x^2 - 10x$

k) $x^2 + 8x + 17$

l) $x^2 - 12x + 35$

Q2 Solve the following quadratic equations by completing the square. Write down your answers to no more than 2 d.p.

a) $x^2 + 3x - 1 = 0$

b) $x^2 - x - 3 = 0$

c) $x^2 + 4x - 3 = 0$

d) $x^2 + x - 1 = 0$

e) $x^2 - 3x - 5 = 0$

f) $2x^2 - 6x + 1 = 0$

g) $3x^2 - 3x - 2 = 0$

h) $3x^2 - 6x - 1 = 0$

It's quite a cunning method, really... but I admit it takes a bit of getting used to — make sure you've learnt all the steps, then it's just practise, practise...

Algebra Crossword

ACROSS

1 Put brackets in (9)

5 You could do this to an equation (5)

6 There is a formula for this type of equation (9)

9 It goes with improvement (5)

10 Complete this shape (6)

DOWN

1 You should rearrange these (8)

2 $x \leqslant -6$ is an example of an _____ (10)

3 $2x + 4 = 6$ is one (8)

4 Some things grow, others _____ (5)

7 It's a type of proportion (7)

8 These are found a lot in algebra (and post boxes) (7)

$y = mx + c$

This is a really nifty way of finding the gradient and y-intercept — you really <u>do need</u> <u>to know it</u> because it'll save you loads of time. Anything for an easy life...

Q1   What is the gradient of:

a) line A
b) line B
c) line C
d) line D
e) line E
f) line F
g) line G
h) line H
i) line I
j) line J?

I know these are a bit more algebra-ish, but don't worry, they won't bite.

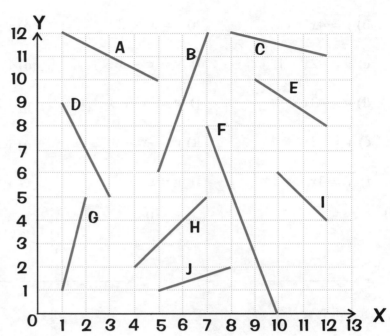

Q2   For each of the following lines, give the gradient and the coordinates of the point where the line cuts the *y*-axis.

a) $y = 4x + 3$
b) $y = 3x - 2$
c) $y = 2x + 1$
d) $y = -3x + 3$
e) $y = 5x$
f) $y = -2x + 3$
g) $y = -6x - 4$
h) $y = x$
i) $y = -\frac{1}{2}x + 3$
j) $y = \frac{1}{4}x + 2$
k) $3y = 4x + 6$

l) $2y = -5x - 4$
m) $8y = 4x - 12$
n) $3y = 7x + 5$
o) $x + y = 0$
p) $x - y = 0$
q) $y - x = 3$
r) $x - 3 = y$
s) $y - 7 = 3x$
t) $y - 5x = 3$
u) $y + 2x + 3 = 0$
v) $y - 2x - 4 = 0$

Q3   What is the value of *x* or *y* if:

a) the point (*x*, 13) is on the line $y = 3x + 1$
b) the point (*x*, –2) is on the line $y = \frac{1}{2}x - 6$
c) the point (4, *y*) is on the line $y = 2x - 1$
d) the point (–3, *y*) is on the line $y = -3x$?

Q4   Which of the following points lie on the line $y = 3x - 1$?
(7, 20), (6, 15), (5, 14)

Graphs to Recognise

Q1 Here are some equations, and there are some curves below. Match the equations to the curves on this page and the following page.

a) $y = 3x + 1$

b) $y = 4x - 1$

c) $y = -2x - 1$

d) $y = -3x + 2$

e) $y = -2x$

f) $y = 3x$

g) $y = -x^2$

h) $y = x^2 + 2$

i) $y = x^2 - 3$

j) $y = -x^2 + 3$

k) $y = -x^2 - 3$

l) $y = x^2$

m) $y = x^3 + 3$

n) $y = 2x^3 - 3$

o) $y = -\frac{1}{2}x^3 + 2$

p) $y = -x^3 + 3$

q) $y = x^3$

r) $y = -\frac{3}{x}$

s) $y = \frac{2}{x}$

t) $y = \frac{1}{x^2}$

u) $y = -\frac{1}{x^2}$

i)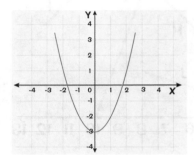

ii)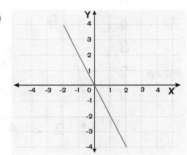

iii)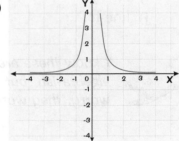

iv)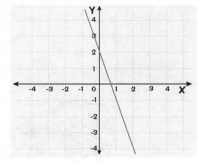

v)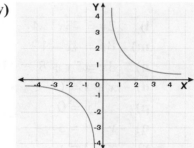

vi)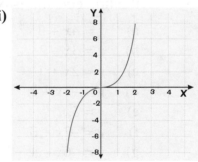

vii)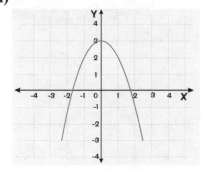

viii)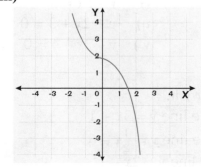

ix)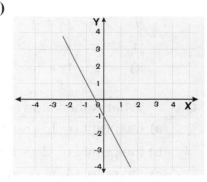

You'll need to be able to _sketch a graph_ from _memory_ — yeah, scary huh. Don't worry — they only expect you to remember the _4 main ones_ (phew) — _straight_ line (easy), _x²_ (buckets), _x³_ (wiggly) and _1/x_ (2 bits and "x=0" missing).

Graphs to Recognise

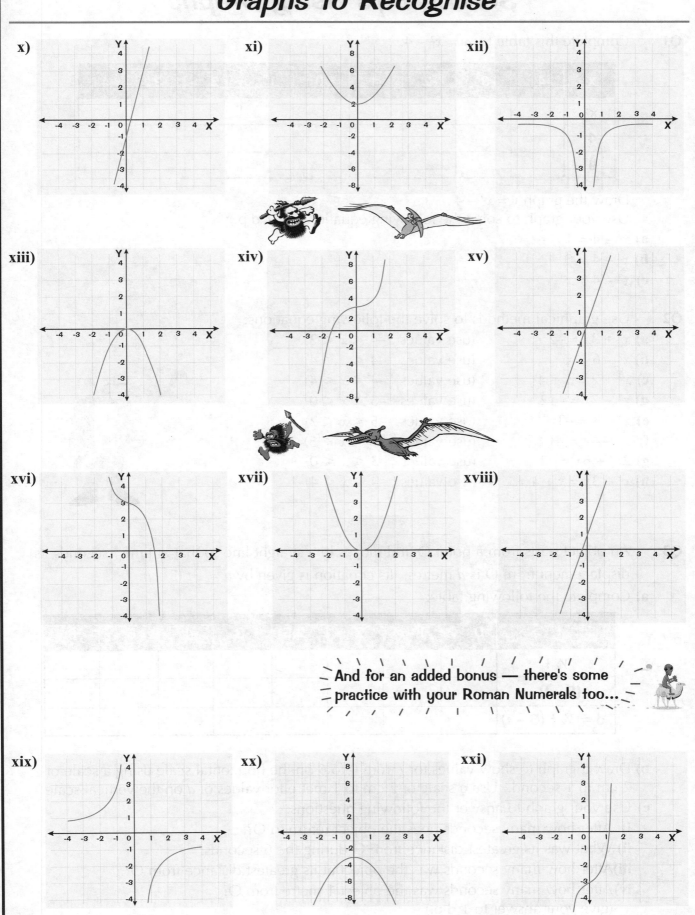

Solving Eq's Using Graphs

Q1 Complete this table for $y = x^2 - 4$:

x	-4	-3	-2	-1	0	1	2	3	4
x^2									
-4									
y									

Draw the graph $y = x^2 - 4$
Use your graph to solve the following equations (to 1 d.p.):
a) $x^2 - 4 = 1$
b) $x^2 - 4 = 0$
c) $x^2 - 4 = x$

Q2 Use graphical methods to solve the following equations:
a) $x^2 + 3x = -2$ (use values $-4 \leqslant x \leqslant 2$)
b) $x^2 - 6 = x$ (use values $-4 \leqslant x \leqslant 4$)
c) $x^2 + 2 = x + 4$ (use values $-4 \leqslant x \leqslant 4$)
d) $x^2 + 7x = -12$ (use values $-5 \leqslant x \leqslant 0$)
e) $x^2 - 4 = -3x$ (use values $-5 \leqslant x \leqslant 2$)
f) $x^2 - 4x = -3$ (use values $0 \leqslant x \leqslant 5$)
g) $2x^2 + 5x = -2$ (use values $-3 \leqslant x \leqslant 0$)
h) $x^2 + 3x = x + 4$ (use values $-4 \leqslant x \leqslant 4$)

Q3 An object starts from a point O and moves in a straight line so that at time t seconds its displacement from O is d metres. Its equation is given by $d = \frac{1}{2}t(5 - t)$.
a) Complete the following table:

t	0	1	2	2.5	3	4	5	6
½ t								
(5 - t)								
d = ½ t (5 – t)								

b) Draw a graph to show values for t from 0 to 6 on the horizontal scale using a scale of 2 cm to 1 second. Use a scale of 2 cm to 1 metre for values of d on the vertical scale.
c) Use your graph to answer the following questions:
   i) After how many seconds does the object return to O?
   ii) What was its greatest distance from O during the 6 seconds?
   iii) After how many seconds was the object at its greatest distance from O?
   iv) After how many seconds was the object 1 metre from O?
      (give your answer to 1 d.p.)

The Graphs of Sin, Cos and Tan

Remember — **Sin** and **Cos** only have values between **–1 and 1**.

Q1

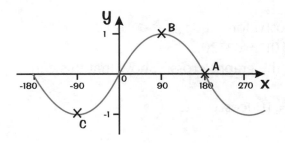

This is the graph of $y = \sin(x)$.
Write down the coordinates of the points A, B and C.

Q2

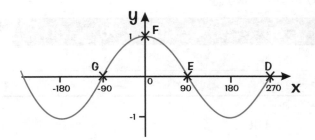

This is the graph of $y = \cos(x)$.
Write down the coordinates of the points D, E, F and G.

Q3 This is the graph of $y = \tan(x)$.
Write down the coordinates of the points H, I and J.

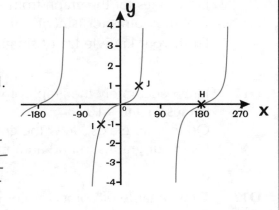

Don't forget — **something strange** happens with **tan** at **90°, 270°, 450°** etc. — it shoots off to **+ infinity**... still, at least it comes back again (even if it is at **– infinity**.)

Q4 Which of the graphs $y = \sin(x)$, $y = \cos(x)$, $y = \tan(x)$ go through the points labelled A, B, C, ...J? (Sometimes it is more than one.)

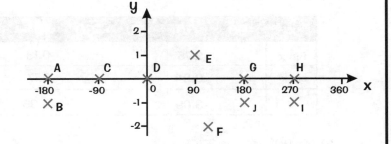

Q5 Plot the points given in this table.

x	0	90	180	270	360
y	2	1	0	1	2

Write down an equation for the curve you have plotted.

Q6 Draw the curve of:
a) $y = \sin(2x)$
b) $y = 2\sin(2x)$ for $0° \leqslant x \leqslant 360°$.

Q7 Draw the curve of $y = 1 + \cos(x)$ for $-180° \leqslant x \leqslant 180°$

The Graphs of Sin, Cos and Tan

Q8 Draw the curve of $y = -\sin(x)$ for $0° \leqslant x \leqslant 360°$.
What transformation is this of $y = \sin(x)$?

Q9 Draw accurately the graph of $y = 10\cos(x)$ for $-180° \leqslant x \leqslant 180°$.
On the same axes draw the graph of $10y = x + 20$.
Write down the coordinates of where the graphs cross. Show that this can be used to find a solution to the equation:
$$20 = 100\cos(x) - x.$$

Q10 Complete this table of values for $\sin(x)$ and $(\sin(x))^2$.

X	0	10	20	30	40	50	60	70	80	90
sin x		0.17		0.5						1
(sin x)²		0.03		0.25						1

Draw axes for the graph from $-180° \leqslant x \leqslant 180°$.
Plot the points for $(\sin(x))^2$.
From your knowledge of sin graphs, draw the rest of the graph for the limits given.

Q11 Draw accurately the graph of $y = \tan(x)$ for $0° \leqslant x \leqslant 360°$. Let the y-axis have values -10 to $+10$.
On the same axis, draw the graph of $10y - x = 25$.
Use your graphs to find an approximate solution to the equation $x = 10\tan(x) - 25$.

Q12 Draw a table of points to plot $y = \tan(x) + \sin(x)$:
  a) for $-90° \leqslant x \leqslant 90°$

x	-90	-70	-50	-30	-10	0	10	30	50	70	90
tan x		-2.75			-0.18			0.58			
sin x		-0.94			-0.17			0.5			
y		-3.69			-0.35			1.08			

  b) for $90° \leqslant x \leqslant 270°$.

x	90	110	130	150	180	200	220	240	270
tan x			-1.19						
sin x			0.77						
y			-0.42						

Sketch the shape of the graph for $-90° \leqslant x \leqslant 270$.
Why did you need to plot such a wide range of points?

Similarity and Enlargement

Q1 Which pair of triangles is congruent? Explain why.

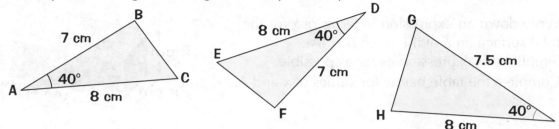

Q2 In the diagram below, BC is parallel to DE.
AB = 12 cm, BD = 8 cm, DE = 25 cm and CE = 10 cm.

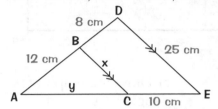

a) Explain why triangles ABC and ADE are similar.
b) Find the lengths of *x* and *y* in the diagram.

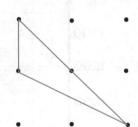

Q3 Another triangle, congruent to the triangle shown on the right, must be drawn with vertices at three of the dots. Show in how many different ways this can be done.

Q4 Two cups A and B are similar. Cup A has a height of 15 cm and cup B has a height of 10 cm. Cup A has a volume of 54 cm³. Calculate the volume of cup B.

Q5 A cylindrical bottle can hold 1 litre of oil. A second cylindrical bottle has twice the radius but the same height. It also contains oil.

a) Explain why these bottles are not similar.
b) How much oil can the larger bottle hold?

 Don't forget that when you're enlarging areas and volumes, there's a bigger scale factor — that one catches everyone out, believe me...

Q6 A boy made a symmetrical framework with metal rods as shown. Lengths AB = BC, ST = TC and AP = PQ. Angle BVC = 90° and length BV = 9 cm.

a) Find two triangles which are similar to triangle ABC.
b) Calculate the length of AP. Hence write down the length of PT.
c) Calculate the area of triangle ABC.
d) Find the area of triangle APQ. Give your answer correct to 3 significant figures.
e) Hence write down the area of PQBST correct to 2 significant figures.

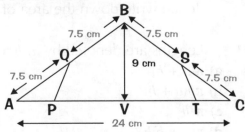

Areas

Q1 An open box has dimensions as shown.

a) Write down an expression in terms of x for the total surface area of the open box (A). Simplify this expression as far as possible.

b) Complete the table below for values of x and A.

x	2	4	6	8	10	12	14	16
A		128			620			

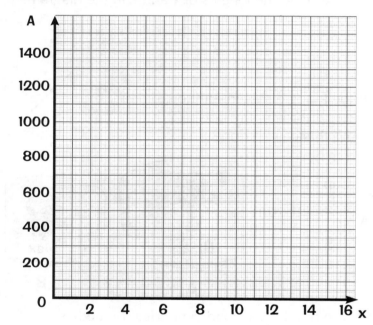

c) Draw the graph of A against x.

d) Write down from your graph the value of x which gives an area of 300 cm².

Q2 A plastic strip is made in the shape shown. The curves AC and BD are both arcs of circles with centre O. The larger circle has radius 30 mm and the smaller circle has radius 20 mm. The shaded ends of the shape are both semicircles.

a) Find the area of the shape ABDC.

b) Find the area of the two semicircular ends. Hence write down the area of the complete shape.

Q3 Lengths are denoted by a, b and h. Which formulas represent areas?

a) $\pi(a + b)$

b) $\pi h(a + b)^2$

c) $\pi^2 h$

d) $\pi(a + b)h$

e) $\pi(a + b)h^2$

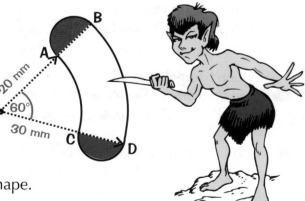

Remember :—
if r is a length,
then r^2 is an area
and r^3 is a volume.

Volumes

Make sure you know the <u>4 main volume formulas</u> — <u>spheres</u>, <u>prisms</u>, <u>pyramids</u>, <u>cones</u>.

Q1 *a*, *b* and *h* are lengths. Which of the following formulas could represent a volume?
Give a reason for your answer.

a) πabh

c) $\pi h^2(a + b)$

b) $\pi(a + b)h$

d) $\pi h^2(a + b)^2$

Q2 Joe buys a garden cloche to protect his plants from frost. It has a semicircular diameter of 70 cm and a length of 3 m.

a) Find the cross-sectional area.

b) Hence find the volume of the cloche.

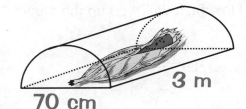

70 cm **3 m**

Q3 In my garden I have a circular pond which is surrounded by a ring shaped paved area. The pond is 35 cm deep and is filled with water.

a) Find the volume of water in the pond when full.

b) Find the area of paving surrounding the pond.

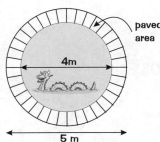

paved area

4m

5 m

Contrary to popular belief, there isn't anything that complicated about prisms — they're only solids with the same shape all the way through. The only bit that sometimes takes a little longer is finding the cross-sectional area.

Q4 An egg timer is symmetrical and consists of hemispheres, cylinders and cones joined together as shown.

a) Calculate the volume of sand in the upper container.
Sand runs into the bottom container at a constant rate of 0.05 cm³ per second.

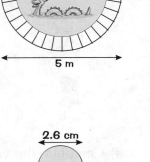

2.6 cm

1.8 cm

1.2 cm

At the end of a certain time period the sand has fallen through into the bottom container as shown.

b) How high (*h*) has it risen up the cylindrical part of the bottom container?

c) How long has it taken the sand to fall through until it is at this height?

0.3 cm
1.2 cm

h

Q5 A metal cube, each of whose sides is 10 cm long, is melted down and made into a cylinder 10 cm high.
What is the radius of this cylinder?

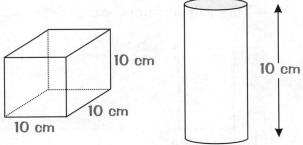

10 cm

10 cm

10 cm

10 cm

Volumes

Don't get confused when they've only given you the volumes of liquids — you still use the same volume equations, but you've got to rearrange them a bit. Go on, give it a go.

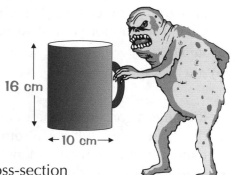

Q6 A tin mug has the dimensions shown.
a) What is the greatest volume of milk the mug can hold?
b) In fact, 600 cm³ of milk is poured in. How high will it go up the mug?

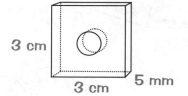

Q7 A nut has the cross-section illustrated. The circular hole has a diameter of 1.4 cm and the nut is 5 mm thick.
Find the volume of the nut in cm³.

(Units...)

Q8
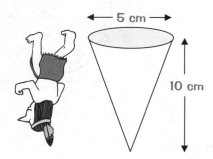

A biscuit cone is 10 cm deep and has a base diameter of 5 cm. It is completely filled with ice cream and a hemisphere of ice cream is mounted on top so that the base of the hemisphere coincides with the base of the cone.

a) Calculate the volume of ice cream required to make one ice cream.
b) How many ice creams can be made from a cylinder 20 cm in diameter and 30 cm high, which is three quarters full of ice cream?

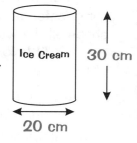

Q9
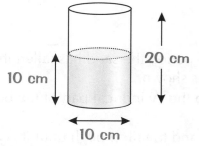

A cylindrical container of diameter 10 cm and height 20 cm is filled with water to a depth of 10 cm. 3,200 identical ball bearings are now submerged in the water. The depth increases to 18 cm. Calculate the radius of one ball bearing.

Q10 Water is flowing into each of these containers at a constant rate. For each container, sketch the graph of the depth of water against time.

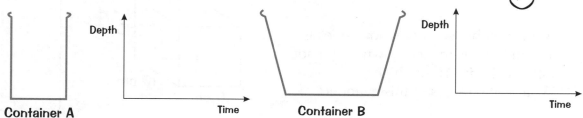

Loci and Constructions

Don't let a silly word like <u>locus</u> put you off — there are <u>easy marks</u> to be had here, but you've got to do everything neatly, using a pencil, ruler and compasses.

Q1 Copy the rectangle and draw inside it:

a) the locus of points 5 cm from D

b) the locus of points equidistant from A and D.
Then:

c) indicate by an X the point inside the rectangle which is 5 cm from D and equidistant from A and D.

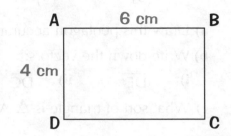

Q2 Construct triangle PQR accurately with length PQ = 10.5 cm, angle PQR = 95° and angle RPQ = 32°.

a) Draw in the perpendicular bisector of the line PR. Draw in point A where the bisector crosses the line PQ.

b) Bisect angle PRQ. Draw in point B where the bisector crosses the line PQ. Measure the length BA.

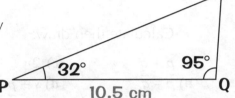

Q3 This is a plan of Simon's room. To keep warm Simon must be within 2 m of the wall containing the radiator. To see out of the window he must be within 1.5 m of the wall containing the window.

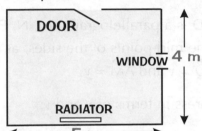

a) Using a scale of 2 cm to 1 m draw a plan of Simon's room.

b) Shade the region in which Simon must be if he is to be warm and see out of the window.

Q4 A running track is designed so that each point on the track is 32.5 m from a fixed line AB which is 100 m long.

A •————————— 100 m —————————• B

a) Draw the locus of the line.

b) Calculate the distance once round the running track.

Q5 The positions of two islands A and B are found from the following information: A is 35 km from a jetty J on a bearing 065°, B is due south of A and on a bearing of 132° from J as shown below.

a) Using a scale of 1 cm to 5 km, draw an accurate plan to show the positions of J, A and B.

b) Find from your drawing the distance in km between the islands A and B.

c) A boat leaves the jetty at 09.00 and reaches A at 11.30. What is its average speed in km/h?

d) A lightship L is 20 km from J, equidistant from A and B and on the same side of J as A and B. Mark L on the drawing.

e) Find the bearing of J from L.

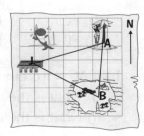

Vectors

Q1 ABCDE is a pentagon.

$$\overrightarrow{AB} = \begin{pmatrix} 3 \\ 3 \end{pmatrix} \qquad \overrightarrow{AC} = \begin{pmatrix} 2 \\ 6 \end{pmatrix} \qquad \overrightarrow{AD} = \begin{pmatrix} -2 \\ 6 \end{pmatrix} \qquad \overrightarrow{AE} = \begin{pmatrix} -3 \\ 2 \end{pmatrix}$$

a) Draw this pentagon accurately.

b) Write down the vectors:

    i) $\overrightarrow{DE}$ **ii)** $\overrightarrow{DC}$ **iii)** $\overrightarrow{EC}$

c) What sort of triangle is $\triangle$ ACD?

Q2 $\underset{\sim}{p} = \begin{pmatrix} 2 \\ 3 \end{pmatrix}, \; \underset{\sim}{q} = \begin{pmatrix} 0 \\ -2 \end{pmatrix}, \; \underset{\sim}{r} = \begin{pmatrix} 3 \\ -1 \end{pmatrix}, \; \underset{\sim}{s} = \begin{pmatrix} -1 \\ -2 \end{pmatrix}$

Calculate then draw:

a) $\underset{\sim}{p} + \underset{\sim}{q}$ **c)** $2\underset{\sim}{r}$ **e)** $2\underset{\sim}{p} - 2\underset{\sim}{s}$ **g)** $2\underset{\sim}{r} - \underset{\sim}{q}$ **i)** $\underset{\sim}{p} + 2\underset{\sim}{s}$

b) $\underset{\sim}{p} - \underset{\sim}{q}$ **d)** $\underset{\sim}{s} + \underset{\sim}{p}$ **f)** $3\underset{\sim}{q} + \underset{\sim}{s}$ **h)** $\frac{1}{2}\underset{\sim}{q} + 2\underset{\sim}{r}$ **j)** $\underset{\sim}{q} - 2\underset{\sim}{r}$

Q3

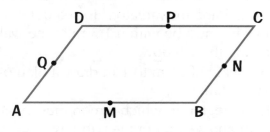

ABCD is a parallelogram. M, N, P and Q are the mid-points of the sides, as shown. If $\overrightarrow{MQ} = \underset{\sim}{x}$ and $\overrightarrow{AM} = \underset{\sim}{y}$

Express in terms of $\underset{\sim}{x}$ and $\underset{\sim}{y}$:

a) $\overrightarrow{AB}$ **c)** $\overrightarrow{NB}$ **e)** $\overrightarrow{AC}$

b) $\overrightarrow{AQ}$ **d)** $\overrightarrow{BC}$ **f)** $\overrightarrow{BD}$

Q4 In the diagram on the right, EB and AC are perpendicular. ABCE is a parallelogram. $\angle$EDC is a right angle.

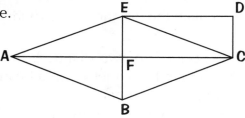

a) Name a vector equal to:

    i) $\overrightarrow{FC}$ **iii)** $\overrightarrow{BC}$ **v)** $2\overrightarrow{CD}$ **vii)** $\overrightarrow{EF} - \overrightarrow{CF}$

    ii) $\overrightarrow{FB}$ **iv)** $\overrightarrow{CE}$ **vi)** $\overrightarrow{AE} + \overrightarrow{EC}$ **viii)** $\overrightarrow{ED} + \overrightarrow{DC} + \overrightarrow{CB}$

b) If AC = 16 cm and EB = 6 cm:

    i) what is the area of ABCE?

    ii) what is the area of ABCDE?

Yep, you're gonna get to practise all that right-angled triangle stuff — Pythagoras, Trig, that sort of thing.

Oh, how the winter evenings will just fly by.

Real-Life Vectors

Look at the pretty pictures... make sure you can see how this little lot fit with the questions, because you'll have to draw your own on the next page.

Q1 In still water my motor boat can achieve 9 km/h. I aim the boat directly across the river which is running at 3 km/h. What is my resultant speed?

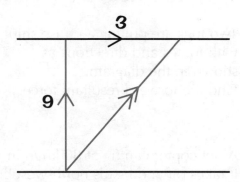

Q2

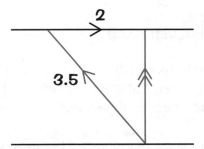

A girl wants to swim across a river running at 2 km/h. If she can swim at 3.5 km/h, calculate:

a) at what angle to the bank she should swim to go directly across

b) her resultant speed.

Q3 An aircraft is attempting to fly due North. It can achieve 600km/h but there is a wind from the west at 75 km/h, as shown. Calculate:

a) the actual bearing the aircraft is flying on

b) its resultant speed.

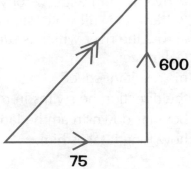

Q4 In the following diagrams the forces are acting on an object as shown.

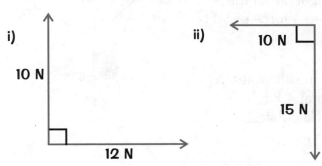

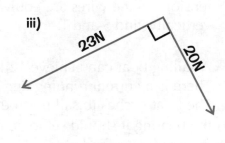

For each find:

a) the resultant force

b) its direction in relation to the larger force.

74

Real-Life Vectors

For this next one, you've either got to split the vectors into components — F COS θ and F SIN θ, or just add the vectors together end to end and use the Sine and Cosine rules.

It's your call.

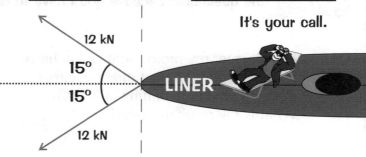

Q5 Two tugs are pulling a cruise ship with forces and directions as shown in the diagram. Find the forward resultant force.

Q6 A helicopter can fly at 80 km/h in still air. It takes off and heads north-west but is blown off course by a wind of 30 km/h from the north-east.
a) What is its resultant speed?
b) If this helicopter wants to fly NW, on what bearing should it head?

Q7 A rowing boat needs to reach a point on the opposite bank directly across from its starting point. It can achieve a speed of 5 m/s in still water, but the river runs at 2.5 m/s. Find the angle with the bank it must make if it is to achieve its objective.

Q8 Two cranes are lifting a bridge girder into place. They exert forces of 65 kN and 75 kN at 24° and 21° to the vertical, respectively. What is the resultant upward force?

Q9 A river is 16m wide. A boy who can swim at 2.4 km/h in still water starts from A to swim across the river which is running at 1.8 km/h. Calculate:
a) his resultant speed
b) the direction he swims in relation to the bank
c) how far downstream he lands
d) how long it takes him.

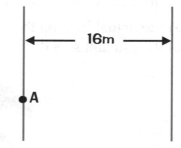

Q10 A Christmas tree is suspended in front of a building by two wires at 45° and 35° to the horizontal. If the tensions in the wires are equivalent to a force of 50 N vertically, find S and T.

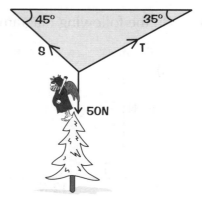

Q11 A sailing boat can achieve 12 km/h in still water. There is a current running due north at 4 km/h. The boat wishes to sail north-east. Calculate:
a) the bearing it should set to achieve this
b) the resultant speed obtained.

Q12 An aircraft is flying on a course of 290° at 350 km/h. The wind is blowing and the aircraft actually flies on a bearing of 305° at 400 km/h. Calculate the speed and direction of the wind.

Speed, Distance and Time

Q1   **a)** A car travels 32 km in 40 mins. What is its average speed?

      b) A train travels at an average speed of 96 km/h for 35 mins. How far has it travelled?

      c) A cyclist travels 12 km at 16 km/h. How long does it take?

Q2   A main road through a town has a speed limit of 30 mph. A driver covers 2¼ miles through the centre in 4 mins. Did she break the speed limit?

Q3   A plane leaves Amsterdam at 0715 and flies at an average speed of 650 km/h to Paris, arriving at 0800. It takes off again at 0840 and flies at the same average speed to Nice, arriving at 1005.

      a) How far is it from Amsterdam to Paris?

      b) How far is it from Paris to Nice?

      c) What was the average speed for the whole journey?

Remember, for the average speed, you use the **total** time and the **total** distance.

Q4   A runner covered the first 100 m of a 200 m race in 12.3 seconds.

      a) What was his average speed for the first 100 m?

      b) The second 100 m took 15.1 seconds. What was the average speed for 200 m?

Q5   A military plane can achieve a speed of 1100 km/h. At this speed it passes over town A at 1205 and town B at 1217.

      a) How far apart are towns A and B?

      b) The plane then flies over village C, which is 93 km from B. How long does it take to get from B to C?

Q6   Two cars set off on 180-mile journeys. One travels mostly on A roads and manages an average speed of 42 mph. The other car travels mostly on the motorway and achieves an average speed of 64 mph. They both take the same time over the journey, but the second car has a stop mid-journey. For how long does the second car stop?

Q7   A stone is dropped from a cliff top. After 1 second it has fallen 4.8 m, after 2 seconds a total of 19.2 m and after 3 seconds 43.2 m. Calculate its average speed in:

      a) the first second

      b) the second second

      c) for all 3 seconds

      d) Change all the m/s speeds to km/h.

Q8   In a motor race, three drivers hit top speeds of 236.6, 233.8 and 227.3 km/hr. If 1 km = 0.62 miles, how long would each driver take to travel 5 miles at these speeds?

Density

Q1 Density = mass per unit volume.

a) Calculate the density of a piece of wood with volume 183 cm³ and mass 125 g.

b) Find the volume of a sheet of metal with density 8.2 g/cm³ and mass 125 g.

c) Work out the mass of a paperweight with a volume 56 cm³ and density 9 g/cm³.

Q2 A statue has a volume of 4 m³. The density of the stone used is 9.3 g/cm³.

a) Calculate the mass of the statue.

b) A full-size replica of the statue is made in a lighter material with a density of only 3.5 g/cm³. What will be the weight of the replica?

c) A small model is made in the lighter material weighing just 5 kg. Calculate the volume of the model.

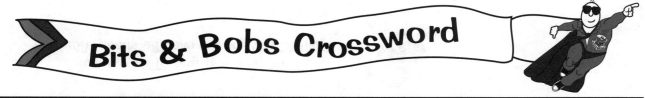

Bits & Bobs Crossword

ACROSS

1) The standard way to learn this is to say, "times ten to the power". (4)
3) These describe both magnitude and direction. (7)
6) The angles of _____ and depression are equal. (9)
8) Unlike a British summer you're guaranteed one if you divide the opposite by the adjacent in a right-angled triangle. (3)
10) $a^2 + o^2 = h^2$, where a = adjacent, o = opposite and h = hypotenuse. (10)
11) A compass bearing due 090°. (4)

DOWN

2) If you break this you may get it wrong. (4)
4) So we click (*anag.*) (9)
5) –090° if you're facing West.(5)
7) An answer is incomplete unless it also has these. (5)
9) Learn how to use this and you won't go wrong with speed and density. (7)
12) Where the gradient of a line on a graph represents either acceleration or speed, you will find me on the axis. (4)

Probability

Q1 Charlton's cricket team had the following results over their last 20 matches.

| W | W | L | D | D | W | W | L | W | L |
| D | L | L | D | W | D | W | W | L | L |

a) Complete the frequency table.

b) Charlton reasons that since there are 3 possible results for any match, the probability that the next match will be drawn (D) is $\frac{1}{3}$. Explain why Charlton is wrong.

Outcome	Frequency
W	
D	
L	

c) Suggest a value for the probability of a draw based on the past performance of Charlton's team.

Q2 a) What is the probability of randomly selecting either a black Ace or black King from an ordinary pack of playing cards?

b) If the entire suit of clubs is removed from a pack of cards, what is the probability of randomly selecting a red 7?

c) If all the 7's are also removed from the pack of cards, what is the probability of randomly selecting the 4 of diamonds?

Q3 For the roulette wheel shown, the probability of the ball landing on each of the numbers is listed in the table below.

Number	1	2	3	4	5	6
Probability	⅙	⅓	⅙	¹⁄₁₂	¹⁄₁₂	⅙

a) Find the probability of landing on an even number.

b) What is the probability of landing on black?

c) Why is the probability of landing on a white or a 3 not $\frac{5}{12} + \frac{1}{6}$?

Q4 The notepad below shows orders for 4 different sorts of rice at a certain Indian restaurant. Based on this data, what is the probability that the next order of rice is:

a) for pilau rice?

b) for spicy mushroom or special fried rice?

c) not for boiled rice?

boiled	20
pilau	24
spicy mushroom	10
special fried	6

Probability

The <u>AND / OR Rules</u> can get quite confusing, so get them drummed into that funny looking thing just between your neck and your hat <u>before</u> the Exam...

For AND, you MULTIPLY (<u>along</u> the branches)
For OR, you ADD (the end results)

See — told you it was confusing.

Q5 There are 2 spinners: one with 3 sides numbered 1, 2, 3, and the other with 7 sides numbered 1, 2, 3, 4, 5, 6, 7.

a) If both are spun together, list all the possible outcomes.

b) Complete the following table showing the sum of the 2 numbers for each outcome.

	1	2	3	4	5	6	7
1							
2							
3							

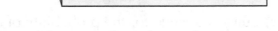

c) What is the probability that the sum is 6?
d) What is the probability that the sum is even?
e) What is the probability that the sum is greater than or equal to 8?
f) What is the probability that the sum is less than 8?
g) Explain how you can work out the probability in part **f)** without using the table.

Q6 3 balls are drawn at random, without replacement, from a bag containing 4 green balls and 3 red balls.

a) Complete the tree diagram below showing all the possible outcomes and their probabilities.

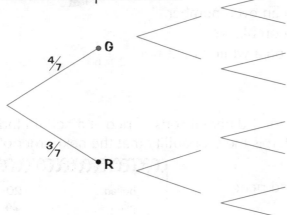

b) What is the probability that exactly 2 green balls are drawn?
c) What is the probability that the last ball drawn is the same colour as the first?

They're getting easier already, aren't they...

Probability

Don't forget the "at least" trick — if you're looking for P(at least ...) happening, all you need to do is find 1 – P(not ...). If you do it the other way round it'll take ages, believe me.

Q7 How many times must you roll an ordinary 6-sided dice for the probability of getting at least one 6 to be more than 0.5?

Q8 An unbiased dice in the shape of a tetrahedron has vertices numbered 1, 2, 3, 4. To win a game with this dice, you must throw a 4. At each go you have a maximum of 3 attempts.
a) Using a tree diagram, calculate the probability of winning with the second throw of the first go.
b) What is the probability of winning on the first go?

Q9 3 coins are drawn at random, without replacement, from a piggy bank containing 7 pound coins and 4 twenty-pence pieces.
a) Draw a tree diagram showing all possible outcomes and their probabilities.
b) Find the probability that the first coin selected is different in value from the third.
c) Find the probability that less than £1.50 is drawn altogether.

Q10 Trevor and his 2 brothers and 5 friends are seated at random in a row of 8 seats at the cinema. What is the probability that Trevor has one brother on his immediate left and one on his immediate right?

Q11 Fabrizio is practising taking penalties. The probability that he misses the goal completely is $\frac{1}{8}$. The probability that the goalkeeper saves the penalty is $\frac{3}{8}$. The probability that he scores is $\frac{1}{2}$. Fabrizio takes two penalties.
a) Calculate the probability that Fabrizio fails to score with his two penalties.
b) Calculate the probability that he scores only one goal.
c) Calculate the probability that Fabrizio scores on neither or both of his 2 attempts.

Always start with a tree diagram — make sure you've learnt everything about them, then you can do any probability question... I promise.

STAGE THREE

Direct & Inverse Proportion

Q1   If 17 textbooks cost £150.45, how much will 28 cost?

Q2   If it takes 4 people 28 hours to complete a task, how long would it take just one person?

Q3   A person earns £6.20 an hour. How much do they earn for 15½ hours work?

Q4   On a map, 2 cm represents 3 km.
   a) If two towns are 14 km apart, what is the distance between them on the map?
   b) If two road junctions are 20.3 cm apart on the map, what is their real distance apart?

Q5 y is directly proportional to x. If $y = 5$ when x is 25, find y when x is 100.

Q6 y is directly proportional to x. If y is 1.2 when x is 2.5, find the value of y when $x = 3.75$.

Q7   If $y \propto x$ and $y = 132$ when $x = 10$, find the value of y when $x = 14$.

Q8   If $y \propto x$ and $y = 117$ when $x = 45$, find the value of x when $y = 195$.

Q9   Complete the following tables of values where y is always directly proportional to x.

a)

x	2	4	6
y	5	10	

b)

x	3	6	9
y		9	

c)

x	27		
y	5	10	15

Q10   If $y = 3$ when $x = 8$ and y is inversely proportional to x, find the value of y when $x = 12$.

Q11   If $y \propto \dfrac{1}{x}$ and $x = 4$ when $y = 5$, find the value of x when $y = 10$.

Q12   If y and x vary inversely, and $y = 12$ when $x = 3$ find:
   a) the value of x when $y = 9$
   b) the value of y when $x = 6$.

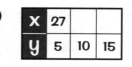

Q13   A man travels for 2 hours at 72 km per hour, completing a journey between two towns. Meanwhile another man completes the same journey at a speed of 80 km per hour. How long did it take him?

Q14   Given that $y \propto \dfrac{1}{x}$, complete this table of values.

x	1	2	3	4	5	6
y					9.6	

Make sure you know the 4 main details about Direct and Inverse Proportion:
1) what happens when one quantity increases,
2) the graph,
3) the table of values, and
4) whether it's the ratio or the product that's the same for all values.

Direct & Inverse Proportion

Q15 The area of a circle is proportional to the square of the radius. If the area is 113 cm² when the radius is 6 cm, find:
a) the area of a circle with radius 5 cm
b) the radius of a circle with area 29 cm².
Give your answers to 1 d.p.

Q16 If y is inversely proportional to the square of x, and $y = 4$ when $x = 6$.
Find the value of:
a) y when $x = 3$
b) x when $y = 9$, given that x is negative.

Q17 If $y \propto x^2$ and $y = 4$ when $x = 4$, find the value of y when $x = 12$.

Q18 $y = kx^3$ and $y = 200$ when $x = 5$.
a) Find the value of k.
b) Find the value of y when $x = 8$.
c) Find the value of x when $y = 2433.4$

Q19 Given that y varies inversely as the square of x, complete the following table of values, given that x is always positive.

X	1	2	5	
y			4	1

X	2			8
y	24	6	2⅔	

Q20 Two cylindrical containers are filled to the same depth, d cm, with water. The mass of the water in each container is proportional to the square of the radius of each container. The first container has a radius of 16 cm and the water has a mass of 16 kg. If the second container has a radius of 8 cm, find the mass of the water inside it.

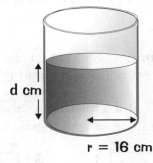

d cm

r = 16 cm

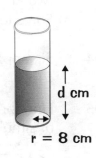

d cm

r = 8 cm

Q21 Given that r varies inversely as the square of s, and $r = 24$ when $s = 10$, find the values of:
a) r when $s = 5$
b) s when $r = 150$, given that s is positive.
c) r when $s = 2$
d) s when $r = 37\frac{1}{2}$, given that s is negative.

Don't forget about that little joker, the "inverse square" variation — they'll expect you to know that, too.

Q22 By considering the values in the table, decide whether $y \propto x$, $y \propto \dfrac{1}{x}$, $y \propto x^2$ or $y \propto \dfrac{1}{x^2}$.
a) Write down the equation which shows how y varies with x.
b) Find the value of y when $x = 6.4$
c) Find the value of x when $y = 16$.

X	1.2	2.5	3.2	4.8
y	166⅔	80	62.5	41⅔

Simultaneous Equations

To solve simultaneous equations from scratch, you've got to get rid of either x or y first — to leave you with an equation with just one unknown in it.

Q1 Use the linear equation (the one with no x^2s in it) to find an expression for y. Then substitute it into the quadratic equation (the one <u>with</u> x^2s in it), to solve these equations:

a) $y = x^2 + 2$
$y = x + 14$

b) $y = x^2 - 8$
$y = 3x + 10$

c) $y = 2x^2$
$y = x + 3$

d) $x + 5y = 30$
$x^2 + \frac{4}{5}x = y$

e) $y = 1 - 13x$
$y = 4x^2 + 4$

f) $y = 3(x^2 + 3)$
$14x + y = 1$

Q2 Solve the following simultaneous equations:

a) $4x + 6y = 16$
$x + 2y = 5$

b) $3x + 8y = 24$
$x + y = 3$

c) $3y - 8x = 24$
$3y + 2x = 9$

Careful with parts d) to f) — some of them are quadratics...

d) $y = x^2 - 2$
$y = 3x + 8$

e) $y = 3x^2 - 10$
$13x - y = 14$

f) $y + 2 = 2x^2$
$y + 3x = 0$

g) $3y - 10x - 17 = 0$
$\frac{1}{3}y + 2x - 5 = 0$

h) $\frac{x}{2} - 2y = 5$
$12y + x - 2 = 0$

i) $x + y = \frac{1}{2}(y - x)$
$x + y = 2$

Q3 A farmer has a choice of buying 6 sheep and 5 pigs for £430 or 4 sheep and 10 pigs for £500 at auction.

a) If sheep cost £x and pigs cost £y, write down his two choices as a pair of simultaneous equations.

b) Solve for x and y.

Q4 Six apples and four oranges cost £1.90, whereas eight apples and two oranges cost £1.80. Find the cost of an apple and the cost of an orange.

Q5 Find the value of x and y for each of the following rectangles, by first writing down a pair of simultaneous equations and then solving them.

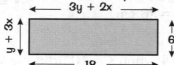

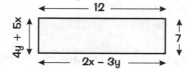

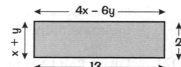

Q6 Two customers enter a shop to buy milk and cornflakes. Mrs Smith buys 5 pints of milk and 2 boxes of cornflakes and spends £3.44. Mr brown buys 4 pints of milk and 3 boxes of cornflakes and receives £6.03 change after paying with a £10 note. Write down a pair of simultaneous equations and solve them to find the price in pence of a pint of milk (m) and a box of cornflakes (c).

Q7 Three pens and seven pencils cost £1.31 whereas eight pencils and six pens cost £1.96. Find the cost of each.

Q8 Solve $\frac{3(x - y)}{5} = x - 3y = x - 6$.

Simultaneous Eq's Using Graphs

Q1 Solve the following simultaneous equations by drawing graphs. Use values $0 \leqslant x \leqslant 6$

a) $y = x$
   $y = 9 - 2x$

b) $y = 2x + 1$
   $2y = 8 + x$

c) $y = 4 - 2x$
   $x + y = 3$

d) $y = 3 - x$
   $3x + y = 5$

e) $2x + y = 6$
   $y = 3x + 1$

f) $y = 2x$
   $y = x + 1$

g) $x + y = 5$
   $2x - 1 = y$

h) $2y = 3x$
   $y = x + 1$

i) $y = x - 3$
   $y + x = 7$

j) $y = x + 1$
   $2x + y = 10$

Q2 The diagram shows the graphs:
   $y = x^2 - x$
   $y = x + 2$
   $y = 8$
   $y = -2x + 4$

Use the graphs to find
the solutions to:

a) $x^2 - x = 0$
b) $x^2 - x = x + 2$
c) $x^2 - x = 8$
d) $x^2 - x = -2x + 4$
e) $-2x + 4 = x + 2$
f) $x^2 - x - 8 = 0$
g) $x^2 + x = 4$

These equations look a bit nasty,
but they're just made up of the
equations you've got graphs for. And you know how to do the rest of it, don't you...

Q3 Complete this table for $y = -\frac{1}{2}x^2 + 5$:

X	-4	-3	-2	-1	0	1	2	3	4
$-\frac{1}{2}x^2$									
+5									
y									

Draw the graph $y = -\frac{1}{2}x^2 + 5$.
Use your graph to solve the following equations (to 1 d.p.):

a) $-\frac{1}{2}x^2 + 5 = 0$

b) $-\frac{1}{2}x^2 + 5 = -3$

c) $-\frac{1}{2}x^2 + 5 = x$

OK, it's up to you to draw your own graphs now—
— still, I reckon you can manage that.

STAGE THREE

Transforming Graphs

Q1   This is a graph of $y = f(x)$.

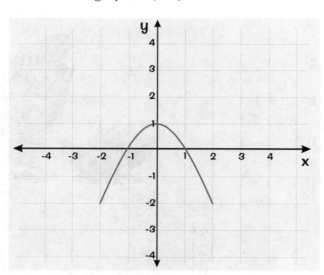

Use the graph of $y = f(x)$ to sketch:
a) $y = f(x) + 3$
b) $y = f(x) - 3$
c) $y = f(x + 3)$
d) $y = f(x - 3)$
e) $y = -f(x)$
f) $y = f(2x)$
g) $y = f(\frac{1}{2}x)$
h) $y = -f(2x)$

You've got to learn about these _shifts_ and _stretches_ — there are _only 4_, so it won't take long. If you don't, either you'll have to _spend ages_ working it out, or worse still you'll _have to guess_. Seems a bit of a waste of time _and marks_ to me...

Q2   This is a graph of $y = f(x)$.

Use the graph of $y = f(x)$ to sketch:
a) $y = f(x) + 2$
b) $y = f(x) - 2$
c) $y = f(x + 2)$
d) $y = f(x - 2)$
e) $y = -f(x)$
f) $y = f(2x)$
g) $y = f(\frac{1}{2}x)$
h) $y = f(x + 3) - 1$
i) $y = f(x - 1) + 3$

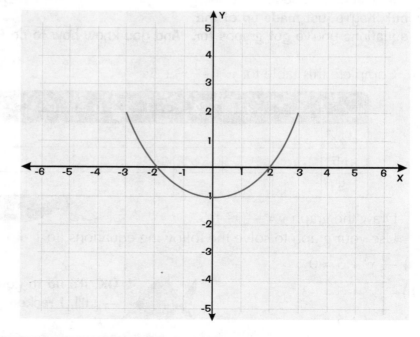

Transforming Graphs

Q3 This is the graph of $y = \sin(x)$:

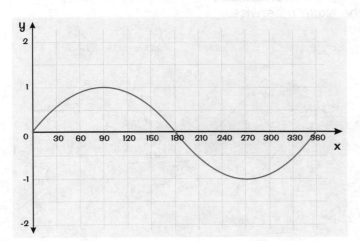

Draw the graphs of:
a) $y = 2\sin(x)$
b) $y = \sin(2x)$.

Q4 This is the graph of $y = \cos(x)$:

Draw the graphs of:
a) $y = 2\cos(x)$
b) $y = \cos(2x)$.

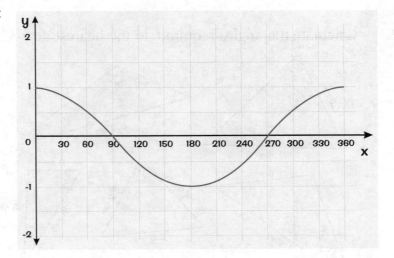

Q5 This is the graph of $Y = f(X)$
Sketch the graphs of:

a) $Y = f(X) + 1$
b) $Y = -f(X)$
c) $Y = f(X + 1)$
d) $Y = f(\frac{1}{2}X)$
e) $Y = f(2X)$
f) $Y = 2f(X)$
g) $Y = f(X + 1) - 2$.

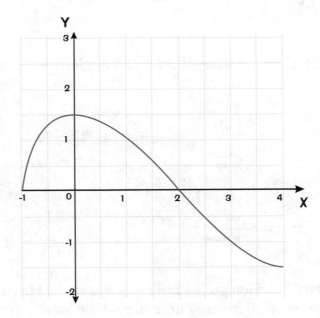

Phew — well, that's the lot on graphs... and what fun it was, too.

The Sine and Cosine Rules

Make sure you know the Sine Rule and <u>both forms</u> of the Cosine Rule. You won't stand a chance in the exam otherwise.

Q1 Calculate the lengths required to 3 s.f.

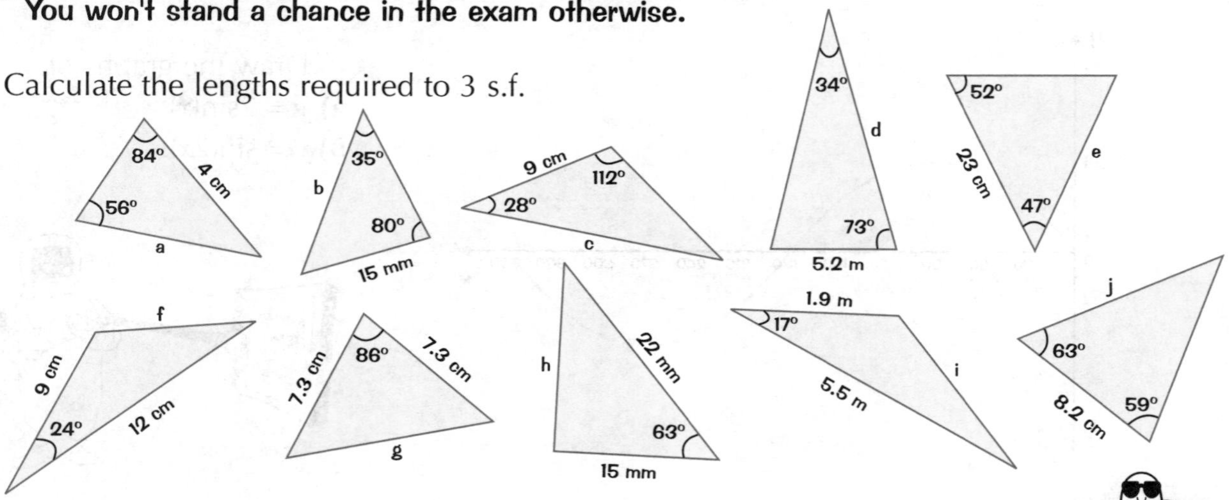

84°
56°
4 cm
a

35°
b
80°
15 mm

9 cm
28°
112°
c

34°
d
73°
5.2 m

52°
23 cm
47°
e

f
9 cm
24°
12 cm

7.3 cm
86°
7.3 cm
g

22 mm
h
63°
15 mm

1.9 m
17°
5.5 m
i

j
63°
59°
8.2 cm

Q2 Calculate the angles required, to the nearest degree.

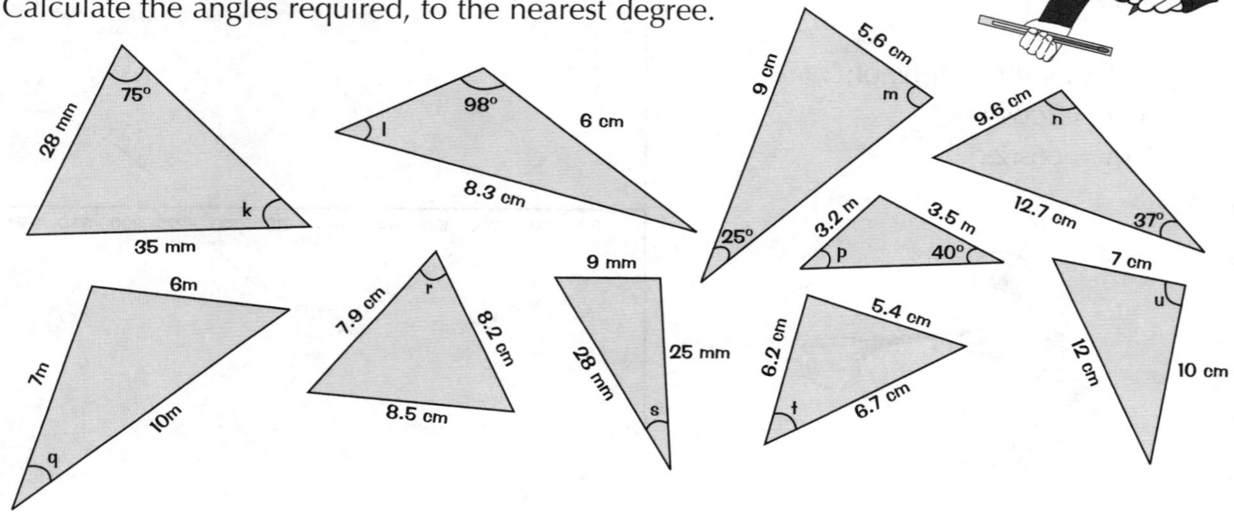

75°
28 mm
k
35 mm

98°
l
6 cm
8.3 cm

9 cm
25°
m
5.6 cm

9.6 cm
n
12.7 cm
37°

6m
7m
q
10m

7.9 cm
r
8.2 cm
8.5 cm

9 mm
28 mm
s
25 mm

3.2 m
p
3.5 m
40°

6.2 cm
t
5.4 cm
6.7 cm

7 cm
u
12 cm
10 cm

Q3 Calculate the lettered sides and angles.

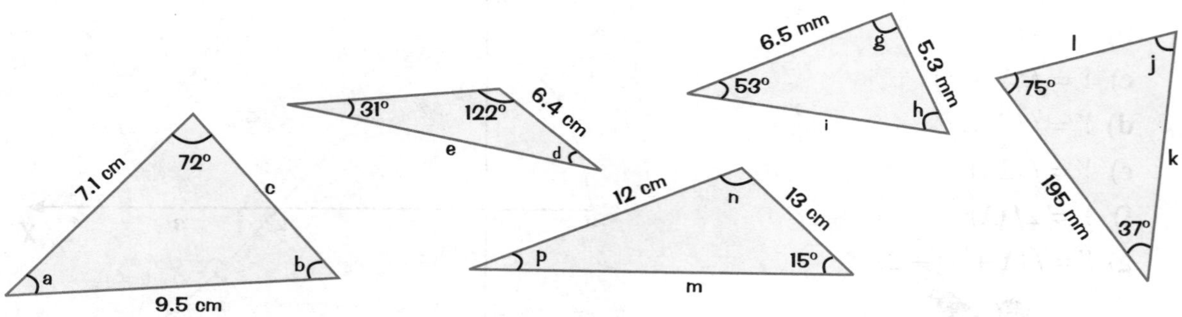

7.1 cm
72°
c
a
b
9.5 cm

31°
122°
6.4 cm
e
d

6.5 mm
g
53°
5.3 mm
i
h

l
75°
j
k
195 mm
37°

12 cm
n
13 cm
P
15°
m

Q4 Peter is standing on a bridge over a river. He can see a tree on each bank, one 33 m and the other 35 m away from him. If he looks through an angle of 20° going from one tree to the other, how far apart are the two trees?

The Sine and Cosine Rules

Q5 A coastguard sees a boat on a bearing of 038° from him and 25 km away. He also sees a ship 42 km away and on a bearing of 080°. Calculate:

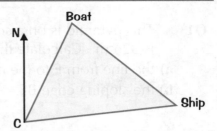

a) the distance of the boat from the ship
b) the bearing of the boat from the ship.

Q6 This field has measurements as shown. Calculate:

a) ∠ZXY
b) ∠XYZ
c) ∠YZX.

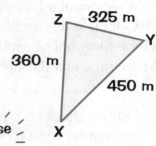

> If you don't know which to use, try the Sine Rule first, because it's easier. Normally you won't have much choice, though.

Q7 An isosceles triangle has equal sides of length 7.5 cm and an angle of 56°. Sketch two possible triangles using this information and calculate the two answers for the length of the third side.

Q8 A parallelogram has sides of length 8 cm and 4.5 cm. One angle of the parallelogram is 124°. Calculate the lengths of the two diagonals.

Q9 On my clock the hour hand is 5.5 cm, the minute hand 8 cm and the second hand 7 cm, measured from the centre. Calculate the distance between the tips of the:

a) hour and minute hands at 10 o'clock
b) minute and second hands 15 seconds before 20 past the hour
c) hour and minute hands at 1020.

Q10 A vertical flagpole FP has two stay wires to the ground at A and B. They cannot be equidistant from P, as the ground is uneven. AB is 22m, ∠PAB is 34° and ∠PBA is 50°. Calculate the distances:

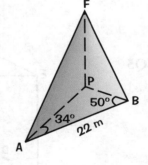

a) PA
b) PB.
 If A is level with P and the angle of elevation of F from A is 49°, calculate:
c) FA
d) PF.

Q11 An aircraft leaves A and flies 257 km to B on a bearing of 257°. It then flies on to C, 215 km away on a bearing of 163° from B. Calculate:

a) ∠ABC
b) distance CA
c) the bearing needed to fly from A direct to C.

Q12 Mary and Jane were standing one behind the other, 2.3 m apart, each holding one of the two strings of a kite flying directly in front of them. The angles of elevation of the kite from the girls were 65° and 48° respectively. Assuming the ends of both strings are held at the same height above the ground, calculate the length of each string.

3D Pythagoras and Trigonometry

Q1 This pyramid is on a square base of side 56 cm. Its vertical height is 32 cm. Calculate the length of:
a) the line from E to the mid-point of BC
b) the sloping edge BE.

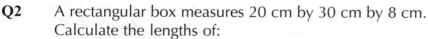

Q2 A rectangular box measures 20 cm by 30 cm by 8 cm. Calculate the lengths of:
a) the diagonal of each rectangular face
b) the diagonal through the centre of the box.

Q3 Rubber chocks are put under the wheels of aeroplanes to stop them moving when on the ground. A typical chock for a large aircraft is shown opposite.
a) Calculate the <u>volume of rubber</u>.
b) Calculate the <u>mass of the chock</u> if a rubber compound of density 1.7 g/cm³ was used.
c) Would a <u>person</u> be able to lift this into position?

Q4 This glass has a radius of 2.8 cm. The straw in the glass makes an angle of 70° with the base and protrudes 4 cm above the rim.
a) How tall is the glass?
b) How long is the straw?

Q5

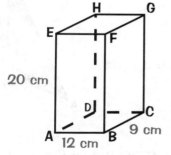

This rectangular box is 20 cm by 12 cm by 9 cm. Calculate:
a) angle ABE
b) length AF
c) length DF
d) angle EBH.

Q6 This cone has a perpendicular height of 9 cm. The centre of the base is O. The slant line from X makes an angle of 23° with the central axis. Calculate:
a) the radius of the base
b) the area of the base
c) the volume of the cone.

Angles of Any Size

Q1 The graph of $y = \sin(x)$ is shown below for $-720° \leqslant x \leqslant 720°$.

Graph of y = sin x   -720 ≤ x ≤ 720

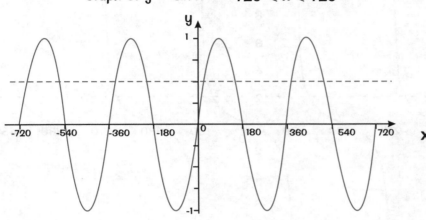

The dotted line drawn at $y = 0.5$ gives values of x as:
$-690°, -570°, -330°, -210°, 30°, 150°, 390°, 510°$.

Write down all the values of x between $-720°$ and $+720°$, when:

a) $\sin(x) = -0.5$

b) $\sin(x) = 0.1$

c) $\sin(x) = -0.9$.

> **Remember** — the **Cos** graph is **symmetrical** about the line **x = 0**, but the **Sin** graph **isn't** — it might seem obvious now, but you can guarantee it won't in the Exam.

Q2 The graph of $y = \cos(x)$ is shown below for $-720° \leqslant x \leqslant 720°$.

Graph of y = cos x   -720 ≤ x ≤ 720

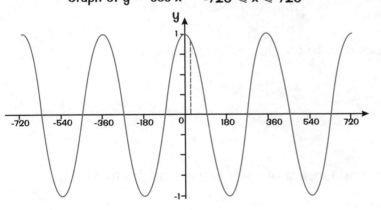

Forgive me for I have sin'd, cos'd and tan'd..

The dotted line drawn at $x = 26°$ shows $\cos(26°) = 0.9$.

Write down all the other angles between $-720°$ and $+720°$ when:

a) $\cos(x) = 0.9$

b) $\cos(x) = 0.5$

c) $\cos(x) = -0.6$.

Explain why the positive and negative values are the same for cos, but not for sin.

Angles of Any Size

Q3   The graph of $y = \tan(x)$ is shown below for $-450° \leqslant x \leqslant 450°$.

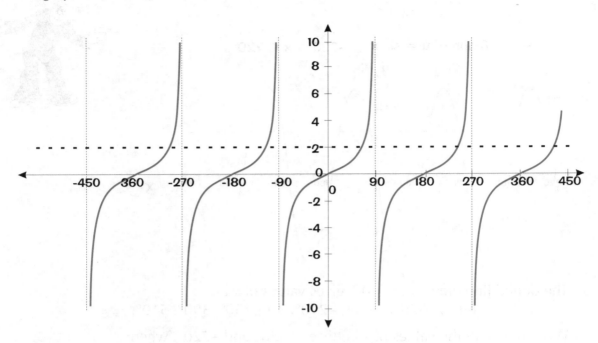

The dotted line drawn where $y = 2$ gives the values of x as:
$-297°, -117°, 63°, 243°, 423°$.

Write down all the values of x between $-450° \leqslant x \leqslant 450°$ to the nearest degree when:

a) $\tan(x) = -1$

b) $\tan(x) = 0.5$

c) $\tan(x) = 3$.

Q4   Write down 4 possible values of x, to the nearest degree, if:

a) $\sin(x) = 0.39$

b) $\cos(x) = 0.39$

c) $\tan(x) = -39$.

Q5   Write down the sine, cosine and tangent of each of these angles to 3 s.f.

a) $175°$

b) $-175°$

c) $405°$

d) $-735°$.

e) What do you notice about the answers to **a)** and **b)**?

f) What properties of the graphs of sine, cosine and tangent would help to explain this?

Circle Geometry

Q1 ABCD is a cyclic quadrilateral with angle BCD = 100°.
EF is a tangent to the circle touching it at A.
Angle DAF = 30°.
Write down the size of angle:

a) BAD

b) EAB.

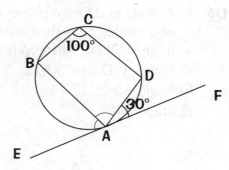

Q2 A, B, and C are points on the circumference of a circle with centre 0. BD and CD are tangents of the circle.

a) State the length BD in the diagram on the right.

b) Calculate the angle COD.

c) State the angle COB.

d) Find the angle CAB.

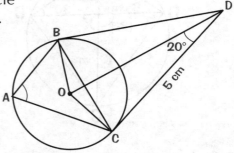

Q3 A, B, C, D and E are points on the circumference of a circle with centre O. Angle BDE = 53°. The line AF is a tangent to the circle, touching it at A. Angle EAF = 32°. Find:

a) angle BOE

b) angle ACE.

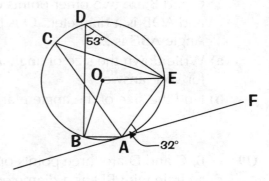

Q4 ABCD is a cyclic quadrilateral and the tangent to the circle at A makes an angle of 70° with the side AD. Angle BCA = 30°. Write down, giving a reason, the size of:

a) angle ACD

b) angle BAD.

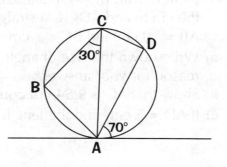

Q5

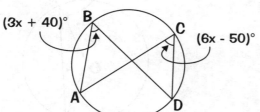

A, B, C and D are points on the circumference of a circle. Angle ABD = $(3x + 40)°$ and angle ACD = $(6x - 50)°$.

a) Give a reason why angle ABD and angle ACD are the same.

b) Form an equation in x and by solving it, find the size of angle ABD.

Circle Geometry

Q6   A, B, C and D are points on the circumference
of a circle. O is the centre of the circle and
angle AOD = 140°. Write down:

a) angle ABD

b) angle ABC

c) angle DBC.

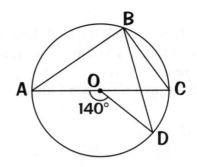

Q7

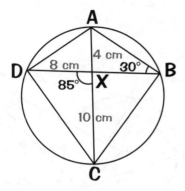

    ABCD is a cyclic quadrilateral. The lines AC and BD
intersect at X. Lengths AX = 4 cm, DX = 8 cm and XC
= 10 cm. Angles DXC = 85° and ABD = 30°.

a) Show that triangles DXC and AXB are similar.

b) Find the length of XB.

c) Write down the size of angle BDC.

Q8   A tangent of a circle is drawn, touching it at A.
C and B are two other points on the circumference
and AOB is a diameter. O is the centre of the circle.
Angle ABC is 23°.

a) Write down the size of angle ACB, giving a reason
for your answer.

b) Find the size of the angle marked $x°$ in the diagram.

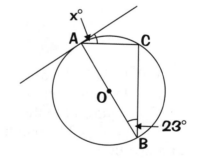

Q9   B, C and D are three points on the circumference of
a circle with BD as a diameter. O is the centre of
the circle and ADC is a straight line.
AB = 10 cm and BC = 3 cm.

a) Write down the size of angle ACB, giving a
reason for your answer.

b) Show that AC is 9.54 cm correct to 2 decimal places.

c) If AD = 5 cm, find the length of the diameter DOB correct to 2 decimal places.

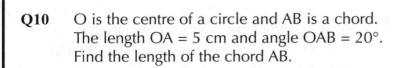

Q10   O is the centre of a circle and AB is a chord.
The length OA = 5 cm and angle OAB = 20°.
Find the length of the chord AB.

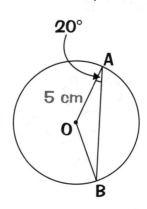

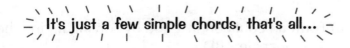

It's just a few simple chords, that's all...